The Magical Empath

Book II

Rebirth & Manifestation

By Lyra Adams

The Magical Empath Book II ~ Rebirth & Manifestation

ISBN: 978-1-7359745-3-8
First Edition

Media info available at www.lyraadams.com

Life Garden Publishing Inc.
P.O. Box 333
Borden, IN 47106 USA

Table of Contents

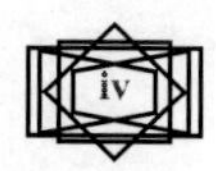

Dedication

This book is dedicated to
all who desire a magical life

Acknowledgement

Many thanks to my current loyal followers and those in the future! I would like to acknowledge my extreme gratitude to God/Goddess/All That Is for life, inspiration, wisdom and revelations.

About The Author

Some say she is a dreamer … and that is true. Lyra is a dreaming empath, but so much more. She is an advocate and champion for those that have been victimized. She is a mentor to those who want to level up on their spiritual path. Lyra is affectionately known as the Queen of Synchronicity because she often experiences events way beyond coincidence. She states her "life is an extraordinary mixture of extreme blessings, divine intervention, and tragedies that often turn to triumph."

To date, her writings have focused on self-help within the holistic healing spectrum. She has been working steadily on an alternative history fantasy series.

Lyra hosts the Podcast, *Breaking Free ~ Healing the Emotional Effects of Sexual Abuse* available on numerous platforms. She is an advocate for males and females who are victims, survivors and eventually SUR-THRIVERS!

Areas of lifelong interest are astrology, divination, channeling, meditation, herbs, flower essences, psychology and holistic healing. Lyra views many of these topics as tools for tapping into her favorite subject of all ~ consciousness.

Join Lyra at her website or any of her social media accounts. She loves to hear from you!

Website: www.lyraadams.com
Email: hello@lyraadams.com
Twitter: @lyraadams
Pinterest: lyraadamsauthor
Facebook: @authorlyraadams
Instagram: @booksbylyra
Goodreads: goodreads.com/lyraadamsauthor

Other Books:

Dreaming Synchronicity: Journey of an Empath
Bloom ~ Holistic Healing Methods For Sexual Abuse
The Magical Empath Book I ~ Healing & Evolution
Real Love ~ Finding "The One" Lasting Relationship

Journals:

Dreams & Synchronicities: A Recordkeeping Journal

Podcast:

Breaking Free ~ Healing The Emotional Effects of Sexual Abuse

Continuing Our Journey

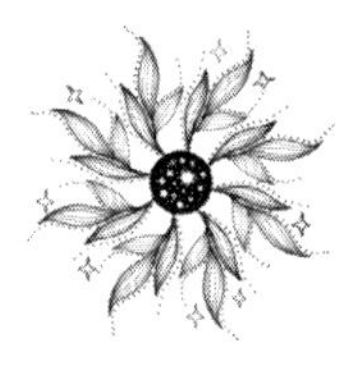

Dear Fellow Empath,

Many of us want the icing on the cake. We want to be able to create or manifest to our heart's desire. There is nothing wrong with this deep yearning. This second book for empathic souls shares the life affirming, dynamic ways you can more fully actualize the magical personality that was always there. I am speaking of the you that desires to use skills to intentionally and consciously create your precious reality. To be taught or reminded again is nothing more than a remembering of what you already inherently knew. You hear the concepts and they ring true for you. You may say to yourself, "I always had a feeling it was that way."

Over thousands of years, there have been many in positions of leadership who tried to convince the peasants otherwise. We were told things such as it is more pious to be poor and that God himself would favor those who lived in an impoverished state. In today's geopolitical climate, it still happens now.

The book, *The Secret* by Rhonda Byrne, made its debut in 2006 and was a huge success because people genuinely want to know: Is there a secret to creating your life the way you would really like it to be? Yes, there are several secrets to not only read and know, but also to implement with strategies. Prior to the success of Ms. Byrne's book, *Think & Grow Rich* by Napoleon Hill debuted in 1936. Numerous financially

independent and successful entrepreneurs have utilized the principles therein to change the way they thought and create riches beyond what many people can imagine.

The bottom line is that these techniques do work — but you have to use them. You have to go through the motions to take control of your destiny. This always includes internal changes to our thinking and ways of living. There are so many books, podcasts, movies and more about creating abundance, that it is difficult to select one. In the back of a person's mind, they are often thinking "which one really works"? Which book will tell me exactly what I am missing here to make this happen for myself?

As an empath, you are running high octane fuel in your system compared to many, allowing you to even create on demand quickly. The biggest secret that you do not always allow yourself to know is that you are steadily creating all the time! The variable here is what you are manifesting. It can go either way — up/down — hot/cold — good/bad — calamity/accomplishment - crash/boom - loss/gain, etcetera. There is also a secret reason why empaths have the capacity to be more adept at reality creation and we will go into that in depth within this writing. I want you to truly be able to take advantage of your God given ability to co-create with the Great Creator. Our loving Creator made us in its image, gifting us with the ability to create, recreate and co-create with each other and with the divine assistance of this loving God force. I hope that all religions can hear or read these words and will find the information to be in alignment with many of their core teachings.

You may be reading or listening to these words on your phone. You might be destitute and at your wits end. You may have created a lot of great things and lost them. You may have hit a certain area in life and are ready to level up. It does not matter who you are or your current station in life, taking hold of your future is within your power. This is true for all humans, not just empaths, lightworkers, starseeds, indigo, crystal, or rainbow souls. All of us have the capacity to create with our minds … for good or bad and however you perceive that.

How do we get back to consciously doing this and living our better life? Swallow now and accept that you might have more work to do internally and changes to make externally. All of these changes are beneficial for your mind, body and spirit. This is how transformation occurs. They are what will propel you to manifest the destiny you desire and, often, one richer in meaning than you imagined.

This second book will revisit some concepts we need to be reminded of frequently. The world of duality we live in can seem so solid and real causing us to often lose our grip on the vastness of the space we actually reside in. Rededication and forging a new direction through the process of rebirth will be visited as well. This creates a clean slate to manifest with.

Are you up for it right now? Can you go along with me and take it step by step? Confidentially, I will admit that I need perpetual practice at manifesting my best life. I fall off the wagon and get distracted along the way. You see, I have consciously manifested physical items and incredible relationships in my life. These are common things many people want such as building a dream home, finding the perfect mate, and making money. During my adult years, I created several businesses of which some were very successful and others not so much. I have experienced physical healing for myself and those I care about. Large sums of money I needed came to me in the nick of time by the most extraordinary means.

Unconsciously, however, I have manifested trouble in relationships, severe lack of money, jobs I hated, failed businesses, and health situations. I believe this puts me in a perfect position to share what to do … and not do.

Will you join me in mastering this next step in your evolution? Can we ride the waves together, up and down, high and low and find a way to flow toward our best experiences? If

you really want your transformation to speed up and go into overdrive, dive into these words.

Lyra

1 - Merging With Magic

"We do not need magic to transform our world. We carry all of the power we need inside ourselves already."
~ J. K. Rowling

Deep within your physical body, hidden from your normal view, are millions upon millions of pieces of life. This life is coming expressly into you from an eternal source that does so with great love. Essentially, this incoming energy is life force. If you choose, you have the ability to accept this love and to feel it right now in an expanded state. Within each microscopic portion of this life energy is an entire world that is working synchronistically to fulfill your experience that you call being "alive".

Just outside your physical self, where your skin ends and space begins, you still exist. Look at your arm or hand and imagine that your body actually extends into this empty space around you. While the you that is extending may be made up of particles that you are unable to see naturally with your eyes, this does not indicate its nonexistence. You do not open your body and look within to marvel at all the processes happening there. They remain unseen from your view. Many of them are microscopic and only detectable with special equipment or processes. Likewise, multiple activities occur just inches from your skin in what you consider "space". These happenings are full of equally astounding miracles of life force activity.

This is an amazing process running constantly without you needing to think of it at all. However, when you consciously choose to become aware of this enormous life force energy and the generosity with which it is given, it is both humbling and exhilarating to merge your thoughts and feelings with this great force of love. When you engage in this merging, you experience what many would term magic. Whether you can hold this state for five minutes or five days is a consequence of the level of desire you have to do so and your inner discipline to mind your thoughts.

Humans are limited with precise language to describe this merging process with immense detail. Being *magica*l is adequate, allowing one word to encase the process and enfold it. We let go of previous preconceptions of magic – those that are affiliated with trickery and logically explained phenomena. Instead, we see magic in its mystery — that which has yet to be fully explained, yet is of extraordinary experiential value. Our experience on all levels of the mind/body/spirit complex is a great mystery.

Often, the unknown qualities of life propel us to question the nature of our existence. By asking questions and delving within, we are provided with the chance of knowing self to a deeper level than before. At this point, growth and healing occur.

Ironically, this is a twofold process of self exploration which essentially becomes Source knowing itself … as it is all mysteriously separate, yet connected. A movement of energy that could be called a dance is always happening. A story of loss, redemption, discovery and love is always being told and can even be heard as a song. Together, we make up this great chorus wherein each story intersects and produces a symphonic sound. Our colors we carry energetically merge to reveal a tapestry of our collective state.

This can be seen on a smaller level with individuals. Someone may write me from another country with complements or good thoughts. Even though they are thousands of miles away, their words and feelings cheer me throughout the day. I find myself feeling clearer on things I want to accomplish that day and work earnestly toward same. In turn, I churn out some of my better work on that date where my words will resonate with others and help them as they read or hear them. This is an example of a dance — a magical dance. And it began with one kind word or deed.

Having control of your dance is as simple as the vibrations you are encased by and resonating from your mind/body/spirit complex. It is within your power to direct your intentions in such a way as to affect your experience in this realm. You receive small proofs of this constantly as you think of someone you have not spoken to in awhile and within minutes, hours or a couple of days, there is a communication between you. You experience this when you think of something in particular you would really like to have and soon, it becomes available to you or perhaps someone gifts you with it — not knowing you had wanted such a thing. This is due to the frequencies you are emitting as you go about your daily life.

Many are familiar with the work of Masaru Emoto and the freezing of water. If you are not aware of this man's body of work, I highly encourage you to check out his numerous books, many of which are primarily photographic in composition, to have a complete understanding. Moving forward with his scientific endeavors, Emoto showed that water is affected by all things resonating around it. Different thoughts fueled by emotion were projected upon the water ranging from intense love and joy to anger or hatred. The frozen water crystals formed symmetrical gorgeous patterns when exposed to the higher love vibrations. Conversely, the water crystals formed with the lower frequencies showed a

struggling, erratic pattern of captivity in ice. Emoto easily concluded through various experiments that prayer could affect water crystals on the other side of the world.

Our words and thoughts have impact on everything empaths. We forget that so often though, don't we? We are so full of positive potential if we can learn to channel it correctly. As a last note on this man's valuable contributions, music and visual symbols also affect water with certain styles creating discord in the crystallized pattern and other sounds creating a harmonious outcome (Emoto, 2004). Negative or lower vibrations create a distortion in the physical makeup and structure of the frozen water.

Now if water is so vastly affected by prayer, thoughts, sounds and symbols, could those things be affecting us as well? Yes, of course. They are continually having an effect upon each of us. Some are more aware of it and some not. With our bodies being composed mostly of water, we are bound to experience effects. But, how do we know what vibrations around us are affecting us? It is really a regular process of checking in with how we are feeling. We must analyze what environment we are in and determine if that could be the reason we feel a particular way. We do not live in a perfect world where we can shield ourselves from every person, place or thing that may overload or lend negativity toward us. Indeed, those lower vibrations can be sent to anyone over very long distances.

What about those individuals we might label as evil or at least bad in their ways of living or expressing themselves? Does the same love that creates and generates from God Source manifest them as well? Yes, absolutely. Water exists — at least here on this planet and others as well or so we have heard. Water exists as an essential life element because God Source created it with love. The environment it finds itself in will influence how the water resonates as it matches and picks up the surrounding vibrations. Just as the water crystals become

disorganized when exposed to different, lower vibrations or what we consider negative energy, humans experience their own distortions. When we feel hot rage, resentment or hatred, we are experiencing a distortion of the love that makes us who we are. Envy and jealousy are a distortion as well as feeling you do not deserve or can't win at something. These energetic thoughts are negatively bent to a lower vibration that distorts the love you generously receive but are bending the signal of. God gives. We receive. How we receive that is of our own free will. To have that knowledge and learn to be cognizant of it is our path toward the magical way of living in love and light.

In almost every chapter of this book, ideas will be offered and explored that can assist anyone in navigating day to day around these issues. However, it does require some diligence and observation. A few of those skills were offered in *The Magical Empath Book I - Healing & Evolution* as well. I highly recommend you begin at Book I as it is a major point of reflection on what it means to be an empath, unique ways of navigating same; and clearing away to make ready for your transformational new self.

In Book I, I also attempted to give a representation of what the Magical Empath was like in their reactions to things and how they moved about in their day to day life. Book II initially focuses on clearing final issues that may be holding you back, rebirthing your essence and becoming a master manifestor who directs their own destiny. While some subjects will be revisited to try and ensure you have a strong foundation to build upon, they will be explored in a more in depth way showing what the actual effect is upon you.

Let us acknowledge we have free will to experience anything we want by the magic of our thoughts and feelings which we emotionally fuel with a substance called intent or desire. Let us acknowledge that if we are serious in our pursuit of these endeavors that we back it up with action when presented and appropriate. Let us acknowledge this energy

dance is a yang or male process of giving toward. Yet, we are also patient in our yin or female energy to wait until the elements present themselves for us to act.

Magic is always mystery because we do not fully understand with absolute certainty how it works. Life is mystery. Life is magic and it is a gift given to us from the one true eternal God Source.

One ultimate goal we have is to feel grounded, centered, calm, content and in our flow. From that point of existence, even if it only occurs in temporary bouts, we are the magical empath.

2 - Connecting To Self

"The quantum field responds not to what we want; it responds to who we are being." ~ Dr. Joe Dispenza

To be more fully aware and continue to experience heightened consciousness, it is imperative that we look at self first before we even attempt to look at other humans, world happenings, or even the constellations and their effect. If we realize that it is us resonating in a certain manner that places us where we are at any given moment, we can work on the inner to totally affect our outer world and how we experience it. When we accept and engage in this level of personal responsibility, we open up new vistas of knowledge hidden from us before. These events of gnosis may happen in a rapid or gradual manner. Always, they will lift us to another level of understanding, which in turn changes how we perceive things around us.

Stillness. I do not need to write too many sentences to convince most people that our fast paced, stressed out ways of living we have adopted are killing us. This frantic pace cuts us off from our inner selves and our God Source as well. It is of paramount importance to have some time alone to reflect on your inner self. This would include how you are feeling, patterns you see, meditating and more.

Placing one's self in a natural setting is especially conducive to raising your vibration and opening you to signals

from the heavens beyond. Just by slipping away from your job or duties for a short time to a nearby park can be the difference. Try eating lunch beside a tree, fountain, stream or river. Not only is this super relaxing for your entire mind/body/spirit, it can open your mind to new possibilities and ideas. Many workplaces, office buildings and hospitals offer natural spots for workers and clients.

You may have promptings when you take another route somewhere instead of the usual. You might change your travel plans in a way that allows you to see, hear or experience something needed for your progression. Follow these hunches with an attitude of optimism or inquisitive adventure and see what happens inside you.

While I was writing these words, we had an electrical outage. Something like this used to drive me crazy, but I was working with an actual pen and paper. I laughed out loud — no problem. In the past, I would start worrying what I was missing and what I might have to do without having electricity. Normally when we experience an outage, it is only an hour or two. Yet, it lasted several hours. I just tried to keep connecting with myself and realized it was a different, unique and somewhat satisfying experience to have the internet, television and other items out of service for a little while.

Still, I do appreciate electricity and need it to operate in our connected world. I need it to keep my food cold and to have warm running water. Yet, I see how I have progressed somewhat from where I used to be with losing electricity for any duration of time. It is the way our world is built now that makes me believe I need electricity. I sat outside and wrote, watching birds and other animals. For them, nothing was different in the way they approached their world. They have not grown dependent upon electric for their food, communication or housing needs. Their instincts assist them in their own guidance and survival.

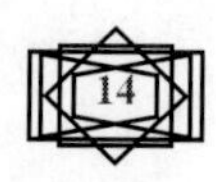

In today's world, it is ironic that our own progression can be greatly enhanced by periodically unplugging in some way from all the noise generated in our societies.

Within *Book I of The Magical Empath*, the concept of a paradigm shift that would happen with our world was presented. Going deeper within that concept is essential now. Some are perplexed at how there can be two or more worlds they have the possibility of ending up in. For it is difficult to see this in our mind's eye and have an intellectual understanding of it. Until recent scientific discoveries and resulting hypothesis have been made, we saw all of us living in one world or universe. Now, many physicists and others believe in the theory of a multiverse. These different layers of dimensions have been theorized to reside closely with one another — almost like layers of plastic wrap stacked together and each sheet containing its own dimension or universe. If you can imagine that in your mind's eye, how hard would it be for two touching dimensions to occasionally merge?

As a dreaming empath, I feel as if I visit other realities. This makes it easy for me to believe in such a thing and in my own mind to imagine that it does exist. Allow me to explain what I experience. There are many times when I am still awake but my consciousness is teetering between wake and sleep. I have definitely not entered a REM state of sleep for I have only lain down for a short time. During this instance of beginning to slow down (change brain state) and drift off to sleep, I see images and hear conversations of others. As I consciously watch this with my eyes closed and through my mind's eye, I see another world like watching a movie. At times, I feel like I am looking through a window and seeing this other world. At other times, I feel like I am walking within it. Here is an example:

I have just become comfortable and situated in bed to fall asleep. I close my eyes and know that I am not asleep yet. However, I can feel myself relax and begin to enter a deeper

state. I can open my eyes, glance at the time and know when this is happening in linear time measurement. I continue to begin the drifting process of deeper relaxation and begin to see an active scene in my mind. One I remember recently was of a cobblestone road and buildings that looked like they were in New Orleans. I see a man crossing the road from one business to another. He is dressed in dark clothing but I cannot remember what style. I hear people talking and feel myself walking down the cobblestone road toward their voices. I realize this is not a dream but feels like I have slipped into a "scene" in another world or time. I wake myself up and look at the time again only to find that less than five minutes have passed.

Is it possible that other worlds exist in realities that are parallel to ours? What does this have to do with connecting with our own inner self? In my book of dreams, some would say the things in the book have already happened and some are in the future. Really, there is no time. Everything has happened and I am experiencing small parts of it now. I live in the now but I dream. When I dream, I fill my book with new experiences waiting for me to reach out and claim them as my "now".

As we do the inner work required to raise our consciousness to higher levels, we change internally on a mental, physical and spiritual level. We vibrate differently and therefore we will only match up with things around us that are close to the same frequency. This does not mean we never encounter people, places or things with vastly different frequencies. Much of the time when we are attracting people or situations we feel are quite the opposite of ourselves, we are still manifesting likeness. How can this be? The Hermetic teachings, which I encourage you to explore, show us that poverty and prosperity are contained within the same framework, just polarized. They both involve value, sense of worth, finances, etcetera. Poverty is at one end of the pole and

prosperity is at the other end. There are midpoints between the two with different values. All are on the same spectrum or "pole" as we will visualize it in our minds. What is the difference? Each is vibrating at different rates of speed. In other words, it is how the thought forms making up their existence are moving/vibrating and how that is manifesting around us. It has to do with resonance. By now, you know that your emotions and thoughts completely dictate your resonance.

Know Thyself

Who am I? Why am I here? What is my purpose? These questions are the thread of inquiry that surges through the minds of all who can think. Some dwell on this more than others. Yet, all ask at some point.

It is a long, arduous journey as we realize that true fulfillment only lies in constantly expressing who we really are and giving forth what we have to offer or contribute. If I could write each person a prescription to begin the healing and revive your own regenerative powers of creation to you, it would be:

Take a ten minute dose of yourself at least two times daily, making sure to know what you are feeling and why. Do not operate heavy machinery or vehicles during your ten minute sessions.

When we know ourselves, "being" takes on new meaning. I am a human … being what, expressing myself how? It is incredibly easy to walk around in a thick cloud, not knowing ourselves and only looking at the deficits we see in others. Our true purpose for our life and the natural gifts we are given to bring that life into its full fruition of purpose become hidden to us and we are in a state of confusion. Often in this state, we go through habitual routines which give our life some sort of structure. This same structure makes us temporarily

believe that the life we are living has motion and purpose. Yet, we are no different than a hamster on a wheel.

Some know their purpose and are working to achieve it, yet keep running into problems finding something that works. This stems from not being aligned or in tune in some manner. This conflict can be from one or more blockages:

- Fear of utilizing our creative gifts a/k/a not feeling good enough;
- Too many thoughts centered around the past or future instead of being where you are right now;
- Trusting and acting on intuitions and synchronicities
- Unresolved emotional trauma

If you find yourself pursuing your purpose, driving up roads that seem like the "right way", only to find another dead end, you must go within more often and connect with yourself to see where things can be corrected. Often, you are not totally on the wrong path, but may need to try some other approaches. You are born with a propensity toward certain abilities that, when combined with developmental action, forge into an activity that is uniquely you expressing yourself and giving to others as you share.

In order to know what you are here to do, you must know who you are. It is not unusual for this to happen later in life. For others, they seem to have this worked out very early and make it happen. How do we know ourselves better?

First, you will need that time alone I spoke of earlier. Begin by trying to get out in nature as much as possible. It is often easier for us to connect with our higher soul self in nature. Allow yourself, however, to learn how to connect with yourself anywhere … on a train, in a plane, in a restroom, at your desk, etcetera. The most important thing is to check in with yourself.

What are you feeling in that moment? Is it anger, gratitude, frustration, depression, joy or fear? If you do not know what you are feeling, allow yourself to just sit quietly with eyes closed and become the observer of yourself. Notice what thoughts come drifting by. Where are they coming from and what is the catalyst for them?

As you connect with yourself, determine what excites you and moves you toward something bigger. Likewise, look at what bothers you and puts you into a state of constriction. Most of us have wants, hopes and dreams, but not clearly stated intentions. This time with yourself is the clearing process for getting into the now, being authentic and knowing what you want to create in your life.

Each time you spend these moments on yourself, you will get better at identifying the who, what, why and how of your life. It will come together for you in a synergistic way through self-examination, creative outlets and ideas, and amazing serendipities that begin to align with your clearer intention you are putting forth.

The magic has always been inside of you. You are like a seed with all of its potential stored in a little micro room of file drawers encapsulated with an outer shell. All you need to do is crack the shell. You do not need to go through every file drawer all at once. Knock on that shell of yours and let some of the life force within awaken. Then, with daily practice, nourish all that is inside waiting to grow and be unleashed.

As you grow, you will sometimes waiver in strong winds and thirst for a time until the next rain. This will make you stronger. Trust and have faith that everything you need will come to you in the perfect time/space sequence. You will grow tall, beautiful and bear flowers for those who gaze your way as a gift you give to others. You will realize you cracked

the question of why you are here and what is your purpose. As you move into knowing yourself at a deep, intimate level, the questions to ask yourself are:

What are my gifts I have to offer?

Can these gifts relate to my purpose?

What is my purpose?

What do I want?

When do I want it?

What can I do now to usher this in?

What do I need to change for this to flow freely?

Ask these questions not only internally, but extend them to be answered by your higher self or God Source. Asking is essential for many times the answers appear or are given to you externally. As you take ten minutes per day to check in with yourself and connect, you will see a gradual transformation that builds intensity and provides the answers to all the questions you have.

3 – Intent & Focus

"I don't care how much power, brilliance or energy you have, if you don't harness it and focus it on a specific target, and hold it there you're never going to accomplish as much as your ability warrants." ~ Zig Ziglar

How easily can you focus? How precision pointed is your intent? Ask anyone who practices any type of mental discipline and they will tell you these two key ingredients are essential for optimum outcomes. Remember, we are all constantly manifesting, but are we doing it consciously?

You need some sort of silence to be a writer. Whether you sit in nature and only have those natural sounds as your background or the fusion of voices and glasses clinking together in a café. One thing I have found about myself is that I like to stay plugged into information. I listen to a variety of podcasts while performing activities that are often repetitive such as washing dishes or folding laundry. I have been known to listen to an audio book while gardening. I will even read pages of a book while cooking.

Always, I desire to learn or hear about something I am interested in. While I appreciate this about myself, I have noted there comes a time when I have to find my silence and sit with me. I have to pay attention to what I think and feel so I can determine where is it coming from? I have to find a quiet place that is mine in order to create what I want … whether that is

creating my next book or manifesting something else. Creating your world is the same way.

There is so much opportunity to allow chaotic negativity to enter our thoughts and distract us from our own personal purpose. We are affected by this daily, sometimes moment by moment. This is why it is important to know yourself as spoken of before and to be aware of what you are feeling. Remember the water and the patterns it will take on internally based upon its environment.

Everyone listening to or watching media now is being highly influenced by thoughts of fear and negativity. Many young people are looking at the chaos and upheaval in our world, wondering what their future will hold, or even if they will have a future on this planet. I believe they will. I believe they will create their future, just as we are all creating the present moment. We are caught up in a divine magical system that is hard for us to comprehend in its totality.

Numerous systems that have been created on earth collectively by humans are busting up and being torn down. The earth itself is showing much of this turmoil in its responses. Monetary systems are failing, along with family, political, religious and more. Family will still be part of human life in the near future, but it may look and feel different. I am not sure that is positive or negative. Like many things, I am sure it will be comprised of excesses on both ends of the spectrum.

Everything is changing around us and we are continually transforming as well, the speed determined by our intent and focus. As empaths, is it possible we can assist in the painful contractions this world is going through?

Let us explore this statement: Intent and focus reduce suffering. How could that be true or not?

With a service to others attitude where we think of all as our family and the earth as something we should be true stewards of, our attitude not only shifts it becomes broader. If a certain critical percentage of humans held this intent and focus, it could easily bring about a more beautiful world where wars, excess pollution, garbage and corruption fall away. We change the future and our children's destinies by the choices we make now and in every moment going forward. We also change it by what we focus on with our thoughts.

Instead of allowing our thoughts to control our emotions and actions, it would be essential to start controlling our focused attention. We can achieve this easily by just being cognizant and aware of what we are thinking and feeling. Again, this goes back to self introspection and knowing self. Each us of is critical to healing ourselves, families, communities and world. It begins small with the self and expands from there in a giant circle of influence, camaraderie and love.

We can stay in uncontrolled thinking if we desire, allowing our subconscious and fears to willy nilly affect our existence. If we do this, we remain aware now that it is building walls, if not a prison, around the individual. How do we know this? Because when we are not controlling how we think, we lose control over how we feel. This allows the subconscious to dictate our experience. Learning this takes time. Some are closer to it than they realize. This is a practice toward mastery.

Once you have mastered controlling what you are thinking and noticing what holds your attention, then you can invoke the emotions you want to associate with the thoughts. Most, if not all of us, have common programs running at a subconscious level. Here is an example:

You are getting ready to meet someone for the first time at a restaurant for lunch. This meeting could be for friendship, romance, or business. While choosing your clothing to wear and grooming yourself, you feel anxious. You take 3 deep breaths and check in with yourself on how you are feeling. Silently, you admit that you feel afraid and anxious … you may also term it as worry. What is the core belief behind those feelings? It is most likely that you do not feel good enough. There is an old program running in your subconscious that states there is something flawed and defective about you and the person you are meeting may see it. Just being aware that you are feeling not good enough is great. You are healing when you know this much.

Now, where do you need to move your attention? Off yourself. Move your attention to who you are meeting. What do you have to offer them in the way of friendship, romance or business? What can you contribute to the situation? Since you are meeting for the first time, you are not sure you want to further the relationship yet. Just start thinking, however, about how you can put them at ease. Tell them a great story that sits close to your heart. Offer your product and its benefits or your particular expertise to assist them. Think of three questions you will have for this person that you truly want to know.

If you meet with this person and they feel you are focused on them plus you have something they want, that works for them. Now you will have to explore if you want to move forward in doing business with them. You will know if you have an attraction for romance with them at this point or not. You will be in a position to ask them questions and find out if you want to nurture this friendship.

Perhaps you meet and both find that this is not working and you have nothing more to offer than a smile at lunch and perhaps pick up the tab. You can both part ways knowing that you entered confident with what you have to offer and if it does not fit this time, it does not matter. Certainly, it does not mean

you are not good enough. They may leave the lunch thinking of another person your product would be perfect for or who would possibly be your next new romance. You have shifted everything inside of you by controlling your thoughts and shifting your focus. You resonate differently by doing this.

Another example:

If I am requested to speak to an audience and I spend so much time worrying about what flaw they may see in me, i.e., "Oh I can't believe she wears those shoes. I didn't realize she was that old." You get the point! If I enter into the speaker experience with these things running in my mind, I am going to lose my train of thought, not walk and feel confident, not be truly present in the moment with my audience. They will feel that too. However, if I enter the venue being centered and calm, this creates a difference in resonance. If I know that I planned sufficiently for the event and focus on delivering what people want to know/feel/experience with me, it will be a success for all of us. Again, taking the focus off me and placing it on how I will make the others feel and what their experience will be changes not just my own individual feelings, but the outcome as well.

What if you are feeling so angry with a person or situation? Perhaps you are upset about some injustice going on. Here is what you can do: take out some paper and write everything that bothers you about this situation. Put all of your thoughts and feelings on this paper. Draw crude pictures of how you feel or what you don't like. Make some of the words large for emphasis. Spelling and grammar do not matter for this exercise. Feel what you have in your mind and get it down on the paper. Who else is involved? Are they doing something or not doing something that contributes to your distraught feelings? Write until you cannot think of another thing to say on the subject. Walk away for a bit and see if you later come

up with more things to add. When you feel complete with all that could be said about this, write these words at the end:

"What am I going to do about this?"

Congratulations! You just slipped into the driver's seat. You are now the train conductor. You will now change this by figuring out exactly what you can do about it as an individual person. This also helps you clear out and know what you do not want. Next, forget everything that you wrote. In fact, destroy it.

Once you have made the decision about what you can personally do about this situation and chosen to take that action or not, the subject is over for you. If you remain taking no action at all, then you do not really want change. You are choosing to stay in the situation, even if it is a global situation you feel you have little control over. You can say to yourself, I am going to spearhead a group to make this issue known and then plan your actions around that. You can simply decide you are going to meditate and send love and peace to the planet and its inhabitants. Whatever your choice, you are choosing how you respond and you are now in the driver's seat with the situation as it applies to you. Remember, it is a practice toward mastery to control your attention or focus, then enter into a feeling or invoke emotions to support your new aware thinking.

For years now, I have focused on trying to stop negative self-talk in its tracks. I acknowledge that it is there, sometimes examining what little fountain in my brain it is spouting from, sometimes not. To accomplish this, we only must be aware of our thoughts. All negative thoughts flow out from us and they invariably attract negativity back to us in various forms. This is an incredible process of mirroring that

teaches us and shows without a doubt where we are resonating with our thoughts.

So far, you can see that you are going to need some time alone, not being lonely, but working on knowing yourself intimately to be the best you. You need time to think, feel, do and test what is working and what is not. You will find that soon you can do this so quickly, on the fly …. And some of you are there already. However, it is a skill that you learn. When you first learn to ride a bike, you are wobbly, going slow, falling down a few times and getting scraped. You don't give up and you keep trying. You pick up some speed and are feeling more confident. Finally, you are in Jedi mode with your bike. Look: no hands! The same will be true for working with your focus and intent. It just comes down to wanting this, going within and doing the practices.

Notes – Thoughts – Ideas – Affirmations – Dreams

4 – Mood Master

"I am sure there is magic in everything, only we have not sense enough to get hold of it and make it do things for us."
~ Frances Hodgson Burnett, *The Secret Garden*

There are so many things that can interfere with our ability to keep a good mood or shift from a negative one. Physical things such as certain foods, hormones, blood sugar levels, alcohol or drugs consumed and more have an effect. Trauma we may endure at the hands of others where we have suddenly found ourselves victims of someone or something affects things at the incident and often for many years beyond. Turmoil created at the hands of another who hurt our feelings, abandoned us, abused us, took us for granted and more can begin to create a little cabinet full of infractions in our heart that we carry around. So we have actual physical hurt, emotional and even spiritual infringements that can affect our moods. Most of the time, however, it is us.

Moods should be temporary in nature. A few years ago, I watched a video by Dr. Joe Dispenza who basically said that when a "mood" goes on too long, it becomes part of the personality. This important point will be covered more in speaking about the negative ego and how it gets its claws into us at times and won't let go.

It is incredibly easy to be affected by the moods of others as an empath. Ideally, our good vibes need to be rubbing

off on others. So often, it just does not turn out that way. Instead, we find ourselves sitting with our hand over our third eye while someone is talking to us or our arms folded about our midriff to block all their "stuff". Empaths also can become their own worst enemy by thinking the wrong thoughts, which in turn fuels the wrong feelings, thus manifesting the reality we would not have consciously chosen but are living within. There's the key: consciously.

The magical empath must consciously direct things by merging with magic — the process spoken of in the beginning of this book. Invoking the love and light into situations that we know will leave us feeling depleted and dark is necessary. Therefore, we must remain very conscious of our feelings and moods. It is wise to have a "go to list" — either in your pocket, in your phone or etched upon your brain. This list gives you instant ideas on what to do when you need to shift your mood.

Make sure you do not fall into the blaming role. Frankly, that part serves only to control you and keep you from reaching your desired state or goal. As long as we are blaming, we cannot move forward to transcending the person, incident or occurrence. This keeps us from manifesting our good that we say we desire.

In order to move forward, we do not shame or blame … we do things to move forward in the game. Conjuring great feelings of gratitude is a time tested and sure way to change mood. The giving of gratitude concept is one I am sure you are familiar with if you are reading this book. You know it, but don't always use it. Again, it is so easy for us to slip into familiar behaviors. One must actively work to overcome this to be a master of one's moods.

Think of your emotions swinging on a pendulum. Watch it sway from extreme highs to bottom lows and a contentment in the center. The Principle of Rhythm is sacred principle number five from the Hermetic teachings. All things

contain and experience this pendulum swinging which creates a balanced flow throughout. How can you learn not to actually be riding the arm of this pendulum and swinging so much?

As an empath who can access a deep emotional water well of feelings, you have the capacity to raise your vibration into such a euphoric state by sheer intention. For instance, you can situate in a natural setting where you hear the animals, see the beauty around you, feel the breeze. You can do this in person or in your mind at any time with the power of visualization. You can almost hypnotize yourself into an altered state of consciousness that bring about those euphoric emotions you want and need to experience. That trance like state is delightful to your entire mind, body and spirit and neutral to upset or despair. The more you feel one with nature, the more tranquilizing the effect. Man made noises will try to penetrate, yet allow the sounds of nature to overpower.

While it may be impractical to remain in such a state as you go about ordinary activities, you really only need to bring it down a notch or two in order to focus. If you are engaged in one of your creative activities, you may stay closer to this enhanced resonating frequency in order to gain new insights and perform amazing things.

The adept hangs on to this end of the pole, not allowing circumstances to take them back to the other side. They learn to navigate the bewildering sea of feelings and thoughts that are not in their highest alignment through a process called transmutation. This is certainly not a denial of feelings. Be careful that you do not engage in that. Stay real with yourself and acknowledge your thoughts and what you feel. All have the capacity to be changed. Our thoughts can change and our emotions along with them. This is transmutation from one state to another.

The Ego

Our egos are necessary to the framework of our personalities. It is what gives each individual attributes that makes them different from the next person. In this context, it is a good thing. Imagine a world where everyone reacts the same emotionally. What if everyone contained the same information and experiences and processed them all in the same way? What if all people liked the same things? This is akin to being a collection of cyborgs. Although artificial intelligence can be programmed with its own measure of ego or personality, perhaps it is unfair to make them sound totally dull and alike. For our knowledge, we know that it is our ego or personality that gives us the flavor in our melting pot upon this planet. If we are not watchful, humans will be the next cyborgs. While we will have personalities we were born with, we may all hold the same beliefs given to us by our programming handlers.

From a deep level of wanting to be accepted by the tribe or group around us, some feel a need to tone down who they are to avoid rejection. This is acting out of fear. By doing this, we do not allow the entire personality to shine through. Accept the fact that you are as individual as a snowflake or fingerprint. You have come to add flavor, so you must release it. If some find it too sweet, salty or bitter, that is simply their personal preference. Not everyone is going to like your personality. You are not here to please everyone. You couldn't no matter how many times you twisted yourself into pretzel like positions. To actualize who you really are, thus fulfilling your purpose of why you are here, let go of bending the true you to fit in. It always only results in you dimming your own light and delaying fulfillment of your purpose.

From a very young age, we are taught to fit in with one another. Educational systems are designed in this manner. While the personality of individual children does shine through within a classroom, there is an unspoken message to not veer too far outside the rules. Do not move around too much, hum a

tune, or do anything to disturb the group. Certainly, in a busy, large classroom, it is best not to infringe upon others. There is a balance here that must be achieved, honoring individuality and not encouraging sameness. Allow me to say that I do not feel the teachers encourage this as much as the curriculum they may be required to teach. Another aspect of this is the usual peer pressure that children and adolescents experience with one another.

Think of the story of *Winnie The Pooh*. Each character has quite a different personality. There is bouncy, happy Tigger; inquisitive Piglet, worried and fussy Rabbit, wise Owl and polite Pooh always on a quest for honey. How would the story change if all characters tried to emulate each other? Their adventures together, as they discover the world, would fall flat.

Our ego only becomes negative when it is working against us. How can we know if we are dealing with the negative ego? Signs are not always clear but clues can be observed when we hear our self-talk say things to us that are negative.

Within each of us resides a powerful spiritual being and a human ego that holds fear. These emotions show up as being judgmental to self and others. They also can appear as fiercely competitive or critical. Fear drives all of these behaviors. Fear of not being good enough, not having or living in lack of some sort. Many stress responses are caused by lack thoughts born out of fears. When we run into a troubling situation, we gravitate toward what we perceive is a safe or familiar setting for us. Our life choices are often based on sets of pre-conceived ideas, images and societal expectations.

By dimming and transforming the voice of your negative ego, you can experience a transition to a higher level. The most effective way to do this is with practices that show the ego it is dead wrong. It takes observation of what the negative ego is saying inside your head. It takes consistency

and some time. If there is a magic bullet that makes this happen faster, it would be the regular use of affirmations and perhaps other modalities such as hypnosis.

Self love can assist as a bridge to health and significantly dimming the voice of the negative ego. Love has a unique way of healing all conditions, emotions and experiences. Love works quietly, mysteriously on people, plants, water, earth and even stones. Love from God/Goddess/All That Is is given to us unconditionally and fully, without reserve. No matter our thoughts, deeds or what rung we find ourselves on our spiritual ladder — this love flows freely. Many times, we block it. When we are filled with God's love, we feel intensely different as humans. An alternative state is induced. Alpha wave patterns replace busy beta waves. In a sense, we are tripping. For some, this can be overwhelming. How do they cope with these feelings? What do they do with themselves now? How long with this last? There may be a feeling of wanting to return and "come back down to earth" while experiencing a grand love high.

I believe this is our natural state if we have not learned patterns that are not conducive for us — or if we do not have predatory types ruining our lives. In a way, that sort of takes us back to the story of the Garden of Eden. There was a split that occurred in Eden between a perfect world and a subsequent harder one to navigate. Sometimes, this love high we can feel when we are intensely connected to our higher purpose and the great Creator can encourage us to indulge in various forms of self sabotage. We may use chemicals to change the feeling in the form of drugs, alcohol, nicotine or food. We may begin to worry and create anxiety for ourselves projecting fears into the future instead of being in our now beautiful, high love.

What if we allowed the love to fill us and stay as long as possible? What if we were exuberant and joyfully childlike with our feelings we were experiencing? That would make a different reality for us — one we might say we desire, but are

sometimes quietly and unknowingly afraid of. This is why so much self-examination and clearing of the old to make way for your new magical life must occur. Grabbing a large invisible rope and lassoing that negative voice inside of us is a major step toward this — major!

Notes – Thoughts – Ideas – Affirmations – Dreams

5 – Feelings of Greatness

"One of the most tragic things I know about human nature is that all of us tend to put off living. We are all dreaming of some magical rose garden over the horizon instead of enjoying the roses that are blooming outside our windows today." ~ Dale Carnegie

At times, you may have experienced feelings of greatness inside or the potential for same. This could be a feeling that welled up inside of you out of the blue or perhaps you just hit a major goal, milestone or achievement. You felt wonderful inside and there is nothing wrong with this at all. It is not narcissistic or egotistical. Everyone should feel proud inside and full of further great potential. You may have also caught yourself shutting this feeling down. So often, something switches in the brain as the negative ego makes its appearance. Its incorrect messages might be that you should never be boastful, stay humble or do not be too full of yourself. What if the truth actually is contained within your original feeling and thoughts? Perhaps you are meant for something or many things quite special. Will you allow the negative ego to squash that new reality? This is why it is super important to recognize this aspect of yourself.

From *The Magical Empath Book I:*

> *"For a less mature empath, we may see them staying in feelings of self-pity and personal*

torment. This is also a passage into egocentric thinking. How can we know that? Look for payoffs. What emotional or physical payoff is the empath receiving to be in that state of mind? Is it poor me? This serves the negative ego and keeps the empath away from their greater purpose and being a light to others. It may reflect a personal drama they are playing out from past experiences ... or even past lives. This needs to be acknowledged, recognized and worked on in order to progress."

What is meant by a passage into egocentric thinking? When I wrote those words, I saw the hamster wheel we can find ourselves on by limiting ourselves to messages from the subconscious that are demeaning, limiting, moving toward lack thinking, etcetera. Sometimes, this has become such a part of our existence we do not realize it. It started out as an event or feeling which boiled for a long time on the cook top and finally became a stew. We sat in our own stew creation for a long enough time that it eventually became a way of operating and moving about in our world. We keep doing it because if we don't, we miss our emotional payoff we unconsciously expect to receive. The emotional payoff is what supports the very deep beliefs we hold that we will not yet let go of. These beliefs are different for everyone and traverse a great number of ideas and subjects. Always, they seem to involve fear of some sort.

If this is happening to you on any level, how will you escape the hamster wheel where you keep seeing the same scenery with different faces each time you go around? How will you escape this if you do not befriend this misguided subconscious portion of yourself and straighten it out once and for all? I also related to you in *Book I of The Magical Empath*:

"It is difficult for the negative ego to be brought under control. One reason is because it loves poking its head out and voicing when we

are under stress. We now live in a world where stressful situations are abundant ... more numerous than the peace we would like to experience. This hypercritical ninny shows its ugly head just when the going gets tough, making it even more difficult for us to shut it up or even know if what it is saying is true or not. When we are stressed, we can easily slip into self-doubt ...

... The negative ego operates like a little jack in the box that pops out at our lowest points or even high points if stress is involved. That critical side of us is very limited in knowledge. Essentially, it only records certain things. It then proceeds to replay its limited one-liners each time you have doubt or are stressed. Because you are in a less desired state, you lose your focus to call it out for what it is. It is nothing more than a negative voice from past wounds."

To rid its major effects upon you, become its best friend. Take on almost a parenting approach with it. You are the one in charge of what goes on inside your head — not that little negative ego portion. You have an ego personality that is perfectly matched to who you decided to be when you showed up here on this planet. You have a purpose that is full of great potential. It is time for the little subconscious recording device inside of you to be reprogrammed with so much good juicy stuff that it begins to forget about all that other stuff it wanted to hold onto.

At times, you will need to take the fake it until you make it approach. In the beginning, each instance of you reciting your positive affirmations or doing other things that

are life affirming may elicit negative messages right away from this new friend you are making. Take control right at that moment. Tell it to calm itself down. We are in new terrain and territory. What happened in the past cannot touch us now. Tell it that all those ideas it is talking about are built on perceptions and those change as time goes by and knowledge is increased. Tell your little friend to again take a back seat because you are driving now and you are going to show it wonderful things to begin recording and remembering.

How can you help heal if you do not do this healing for you? The negative ego has been running so much of our lives. We were just not aware of it. The more you learn to differentiate its voice from your own, or that of intuition and spirit, the further you will progress into a magical life. It's really that simple, yet I also understand that it is complex to put into action. It is a day to day, almost moment by moment monitoring for awhile. Eventually, something switches and changes to make it all transform and you are different then — more magical. There are no more moment to moment corrections. Now, you are simply doing check-ins with yourself daily examining how you are feeling, what is being generated around you in your reality.

Beside this major interference that goes on within our minds, there are other forces colluding with the negative ego. This can come from media messages we have seen recently and even over a period of years. There is a reason they call it programming. Whether you are a man or a woman, think of all the advertisements you have seen and heard that pretty much suggest or tell what you should be like. This is a huge influence on culture and people's personalities. News sources that give us programming about the economy, taxes and other limitations and problems certainly can team up with the negative ego. Overall, each facet of society holds collective beliefs that can have an effect on our overall attitudes and the programming that lies within the negative ego. It is for sure

that our family and sometimes friends can create self doubt for us as well. Try to stay out of the heaviness of this matrix composed of lack, limitation, hatred and negativity. I am not suggesting you stick your head in the sand and be oblivious to things. Instead, put time limits on being exposed to things that will bring you down and if something really grieves your heart, ask yourself and Source what you can do to help remedy that situation, even if it is simply holding space for peace, love and tranquility. Pray for those who perpetrate ill will and even evil upon others. Send them love and light. Let that be your way of seeing what is contained within the third dimensional reality we are splitting from instead of finding yourself sick because you totally immersed yourself in the programming there.

Sometimes I come across others who express being grateful for a message I have put out. They might mention they were beginning to doubt their long held beliefs. This can happen when you feel alone with your beliefs which others may see as being of unsound mind. Some went through a period in life when they were quite adept at manifesting and living a fairly balanced life. And then, something occurred to change that. It could have been a sudden switch or something more gradual that begin to take hold. Their core beliefs began to come into question about everything. Yet, this is very fixable for these individuals because once you really "get" this. It is like riding a bike. You never forget how, but you must have your legs and feet working the pedals and believe that you can get on the bike and keep it upright.

During our lives, each of us will be challenged on belief level and have our foundation shaken. Sudden happenings such as losing a loved one can certainly rattle us thoroughly. Discovering a betrayal where we thought we could trust — or hoped we could, can be devastating to our belief systems. Failure at something we were attempting to accomplish often creates a new level of mistrust about things with ourselves and the world in general. Yet, failure is a natural thing that can

move us toward the greater thing we really long for but cannot see yet. Failure is the teacher of experience. It is just a part of the path toward finally succeeding at something larger than what we have now. By seeing failure as a friend or teacher that is guiding us, we cannot get caught up in challenging our core beliefs. We learn from it, make adjustments and roll on.

Each time we engage in the dance of life and welcome its embrace, we find ourselves moving more into the state of being magical. This means we keep our negative ego in check and allow it to take lots of naps or vacations. Our thoughts that we are thinking are the absolute foundation for manifesting. I want you to experience more magical moments of being in the flow, of everything working toward your goals. To do this more often, you will benefit by watching how you react to others and situations. Everything you are learning on this journey about yourself is not just helpful, it is necessary to live this magical life. When you experience the electric type energy of this magic around you, as you go along down the lane of your life, you will finally know why people are suddenly attracted to you and you come across the luckiest situations.

But you must stop feeling like you have no power to change things, being depressed, allowing others to affect you so deeply with just their physical presence or moods. It's okay to acknowledge that you picked up on their crap, but don't absorb it. When you have mishaps, accidents or other incidents that are unplanned and seem negative, stop for just a moment and ask if there is a silver lining here of any sort. When you feel doubtful, just know that is contrary to being magical. Magic requires excited anticipatory faith.

Faith

We have heard many in religious communities lecture on having faith. Indeed, it is a critical component to living a magical life that is connected and directed by a loving God Creator that wants to help us manifest the best experiences

possible and grow in love and light. Can we have faith in something only because there are written words about it? Does faith instantly appear within our mental framework when someone states we must have it and just believe? I think that is a harder road to travel and it will many times be filled with doubt.

One day, I was prompted to examine my own faith in the Great Creator force or God/Goddess/All That Is. At what point did I become a person that would never doubt that God existed? I always knew about the invisible world, catching rare glimpses of it in one way or another from the time I was in a crib until adulthood. Yet, I cannot say with certainty that this is what I would describe as God Creator Source. These were happenings that many would term paranormal but which are perfectly natural for someone when they are open to such things.

My faith was cemented by divine interventions and miracles that periodically occurred. Each time, their signature was such that it had to have come from a divine Source who wanted to shed love and grace upon me. When I was younger, this occurred even though I was so messed up and had so much to learn.

This faith began to build in a strong way as I went back to my practice of meditation and prayer. I began entering the silence once more to hear even the slightest message that might be there for me. I took my gratitude, love for the Creator and all its creation, and my concerns in prayer. Faith was something I allowed to build. I did not blindly say, "I have faith God exists." I experienced God in ways that ultimately may be small, but felt large to me. I knew of God's existence. I was given gifts of clarity on rare occasions and insightful moments that included a type of sight that is not merely human, but to see into another structure of existence for short periods of time.

These are my thoughts about faith --- how to have it and build it. Like anything, you must be open, willing, practicing and thoughtful about it. With strong faith, you are the mustard seed and you can move mountains. One key is to build a bridge or an open communication between you and the Creator. We falter. We are not perfect in our human bodies and minds. Yet, faith allows for hope. Hope allows for anticipated changes. Build faith, however it comes about for you. It is your friend through all moods and experiences you will have.

You are a continual work in progress that is moving toward a more expansive, beautiful experience. Listening to your self talk and the messages from the negative ego will give you the opportunity to begin reprogramming this lonely, discontent portion we all carry within. You can begin to move from doubt, which is the sword of death for magic, to self assurance that is not just making a quick appearance or conjuring a positive thought. Rather, your core beliefs will have shifted and changed to such an extent that your confidence provides a steel framework from which to launch your best life.

Remember that all your intentions you want to manifest are built upon this shiny foundational structure made of thought, beliefs, faith and emotions. It is where you resonate at your core which is why it is so beneficial to daily be mindful of your thoughts and feelings. Most of all, feel your greatness on this remarkable journey.

6 – Balance & Power

"After all, the ordinary hero hiding in each of us is often the most powerful catalyst for change." ~ Tate Taylor

There are times in our lives when we are in particular circumstances, either by force or choice, that keep us from feeling balanced. In the United States, World War II served as a catalyst to catapult American woman into the workplace as their male counterparts participated in the defense of their own homeland and allied countries. Prior to this, many were housewives. These women did not have the extent of machinery or appliances we have today to assist in meal preparation or keeping up the home. If they were fortunate, their mother, aunt or mother-in-law lived with them to assist in raising children, cooking meals and doing laundry.

At least 350,000 women also joined the armed services in various capacities to assist in the war. During this time, people had to pull together. What they had seen as normal family dynamics was upset and things changed drastically, not only in the United States, but in many countries of this world war. In other words, they were somewhat forced into an "out of balance" lifestyle in order to bring about a better result.

The college experience can also induce such a drastic change in balance. Suddenly, you may find that studying so many hours has not only your time for leisure pursuits out of balance, but your body also feels the brunt of too much time

sitting and stressing. This is a situation where you are out of balance for awhile in order to achieve a goal and it is by pure choice.

Throughout the world, people are put in situations that are not of their own making where life is totally out of balance for them. This could include living in an area where war is ongoing or resources are limited. Certainly, during the 2020 pandemic, many people felt their life became way out of balance.

Let us explore why balance is so important to all humans and especially empaths. When you work toward living a balanced life, it is an honoring of you. Trying to achieve balance means you love self. By attempting to stay centered in this fast paced world, you are furthering your path and purpose. While it is not always achievable, the more you can build a balanced stable foundation under you with regard to your emotions and thoughts, the more fortified your life structure will be.

Realizing that you only have so much energy, take notice of how you can steal away moments to revive and center again. For those engaged in studies; taking care of others; or endeavors that require a good bit of energy and time, try to carve out some for you. It is amazing what a difference this can make. It is also part of putting limitations and boundaries on things. Coming more into balance is often the empath's fault for not enforcing those limits. If you do not squeak a little, no one will offer you some grease. Stop worrying you may anger someone or draw attention to yourself that is unfavorable. It is wise to stop caring about what others think to the point you are out of balance and shutting your needs down.

Contrary to what religious dogma may teach, those that do not stick up for themselves do not get rewards at the end. Or, as one person said, "When you put yourself last, the Universe will do likewise."

It may seem like it is good to be so self-less and take care of so many things. However, it can take a huge toll on a person on many levels. It is important to refill your well consistently, not just when it has run completely dry by lack of oversight or accident. Besides, when you feel balanced and whole inside, you stop unconsciously looking for others to fill those empty voids inside of you.

Many times, we feel confused about how to achieve a better balance in our lives with less stress and more time to enjoy pleasure -- even if that is something some would consider work. Find what makes you feel nourished inside because that will serve as medicine for you. Open yourself and listen to the nudges and messages coming to you from your higher self or spiritual guides. Ask to be shown what will help you in achieving a strong foundation through balance. You are not expected to know all information or be everything to everyone. You are on a journey …. one that is hopefully magical for you. Try to keep your balance and be in the now. Enjoy where you are on that path. To rush things is to fall out of balance.

Let us briefly explore the concept of feeling in balance by visualizing ourselves as a pole that has a negative charge at one end and a positive at the other. We are constantly trying to find that happy medium or our center point. We know we contain all of everything that makes up the pole, but we primarily want to find a resting area on the pole that is our happy spot. Each person ascertains that for themselves. Always, it is where you are currently resonating. That is ultimately determined by your thoughts and feelings — no matter what is going on around you.

How you handle the next zombie attack depends upon how you are thinking. Will you fight, flight or freeze? How you handle the winning lottery ticket is based upon the same thing. You are the determining factor at all times no matter

what is happening around you. Things happen, you respond. You are responsible in your ability to respond.

Yin and yang are concepts from earth's eastern philosophies that show us forms of duality in this existence we have been born into. Yin is magnetic and receiving and yang tends to be on fire with activity and motion — making things happen. Within you, these two principles are held no matter your gender. They exist within all humans. Sometimes you hold back and wait for things to happen. Other times, you strike out and make something happen. This is part of the dance — the balance you need to achieve for a great life. How do we know when to do what? Being connected to our Source through meditation and constantly engaging our intuition is one key to knowing.

Questions to ask and explore for greater balance:

- How am I restricting my female or yin energy?
- How am I restricting my male or yang energy?
- What am I personally resisting, if anything? Why? Is there fear attached to it?
- What could I do now in this moment to transmute this energy in a positive way for myself?
- Do I ever set up situations in my life by restricting, shutting down or denying these sides of myself?
- Do I "zone out" too much and fail to take action?
- Am I always doing and not leaving moments to relax, chill or be inspired?
- Would something as simple as a walking meditation put me in a different place and bring more balance?

These questions will help you determine how to achieve more balance between the yin and yang energies you hold. By

making any changes you discover are needed, you will feel more in balanced control of your life.

Power

We cannot talk about balance without mentioning power — personal power — your power to choose, act and be. It is also easy to fall into old roles that we have outgrown. They almost become our "go to" modes unconsciously and we suddenly may find ourselves slipping into victim role for instance. The victim stance is definitely one that does not put you in a position of power.

Our choice of words, both in our minds and those we verbalize, have resonance of their own which blends with who we are. Instead of should, we can say I will or I choose. This gives true ownership to the thought or position and displays personal power. When you hear "should" from another, realize they are only imparting a portion of their current belief system on you. To even give one a choice, to say you know "you could" do this or that is more expansive and gives the recipient free will in the matter. Yet, this also imparts the belief system of the person using "could".

As creatures of habit, it is incredibly easy for us to slip into non-productive roles or attitudes that do not serve us. Sometimes, we choose to react too swiftly about something, whereas if we waited, we could have a more tempered measured response. This more deliberate way of acting helps stretch our personal power. We then move through a circumstance or situation with strength that ultimately can help raise our vibration.

Each time you hear yourself say, I should, replace it with I choose or I will. You may find that you have often been using this word "should" to express things you have no real intention of doing at the present time or even in the near future. This will make you more honest with yourself. The clarity you will gain from this simple exercise will, over time, change you

and raise your frequency. This clearing also will assist you greatly in the area of manifesting your desires.

Typical Examples:

- "I should clean the kitchen floor."
- "I choose to clean the kitchen floor now."
- "I could clean the kitchen floor, but I would rather binge watch this show."
- "I should quit smoking."
- "Evidently, I am not yet willing to quit smoking."
- "I know my health will improve vastly as a non-smoker."

It appears that when our self talk is saying "should" a lot, we are almost beating up on ourselves in a constant way. The message is consistently saying that where you are right now is not good enough. There are things you "should" be doing to be better, have better, experience more.

Our level of personal power is directly tied to how we are resonating in our life. Consistently, what the information and feedback systems show us in this realm is that we must first just BE - if you truly just relax with your BE-ING, loving yourself, your environment, and the world with a childlike sense of gratitude. — you have accomplished the first step. At this point you are well grounded.

The attitude shift is easy, gentle and productive. Now, I should clean the kitchen floor can turn into — Oh, I love my kitchen and let's make this floor clean and beautiful.

The quitting smoking can become: I love my body too much to keep this up. I will get help immediately to correct the long habit I have created and protect my body, breath and life force.

These are examples on how watching what you say to yourself can turn into being more honest about your concerns, ideas and intentions. This act of self-awareness thus raises your personal integrity and you resonate a little higher as well. You also gain strength to tackle things you previously only chastised yourself over and over again about.

Ultimately, it's about speaking truth. Perhaps, you have heard others say that even when you tell a little white lie it affects you in some way, perhaps dimming your inner light. Whether that is true or not, it always can affect your personal integrity. This is how we feel about ourselves at a core level and that is huge. Core level beliefs affect our inner attitudes and the way we project our outer personalities. We leak our personal power when we do things to infringe upon our own integrity.

Anything or person in your life that was your nemesis, adversary or villain that allowed you to experience victimization soon rises to the top as you approach adulthood or even as early as puberty. This clearing away of any disempowering roles that you might be unconsciously slipping into is wise and part of your transformation. It is important to be truthful with our inner self and examine when and where we may fall into these unnecessary roles. There are many varied roles to ponder and look at. Just by being willing to honestly look at self and ask: is there anyone or anything I am attempting to manipulate with my choices, moods, behaviors will open this up for greater examination.

Remember that you do not have to battle your thoughts. You have the ability to change your thoughts as needed to be who you are on a soul level embodied in physical form here. Remember, you are becoming not only best friends with your subconscious negative ego, but directing it as if you are an older best friend teaching it new ideas.

Living our truth is the end goal for the magical empath as they no longer feel the need to hide who and what they are. Through reality creation techniques and the clearing away of

residue from the past, the magical empath has created a world where they can daily truthfully live their purpose … whatever that is. Seek your magic everyday by fostering balance and not giving up your personal power in known or unknown ways.

7 – Challenging Times

"Painful as it may be, a significant emotional event can be the catalyst for choosing a direction that serves us - and those around us - more effectively. Look for the learning." ~ Louisa May Alcott

Do you think each generation on earth over many thousands of years thought they were living through the most difficult times to date? I do not think everyone now believes that, but many do. Always, it is how we are focused upon something and our perceptions of it. This chapter was written to talk about our responses to challenging world events and times of our earth story.

No matter which time line you came into, things are happening and it can be difficult to regulate your emotions, to readjust what you are doing and thinking. Learning to accomplish mood and thought transmutation will allow you to be so much stronger in your physical and spiritual walk in life.

Constantly, seeds of love or seeds of hate and fear are being planted on this planet which is experiencing the birthing pains of moving into fourth dimension. It is up to us to ease that suffering — to be the midwives calming the fears, quelling the screams, subduing the anger of this transitional time. It does not mean we are responsible for the behavior of others. It only means that it's time for us to be clear with ourselves, our own relationships and once we have accomplished that, we are

available to help others. That can be achieved very well, even if we are not at 100%. The important thing is that you see this more as an opportunity than a dilemma happening to you. It is a shift in perception that I believe is more in alignment of why I and you are here.

In the recent past, we entered a time of endings that included a breakdown of things that are no longer working. This has happened on personal levels as well as societal and governmental. This gave us and still gives us the opportunity to eliminate some things and create new ones. This has to happen during this transition time. For instance, you will continue to discover many things that have been kept somewhat secret or underground from the majority. Some of these secrets have gone on for many years. Some are more recent. Some of them may be labeled conspiracy theories and could be so. Yet, some of them may be true and conspiratorial in nature. It will be very difficult for you to know what is real and what is not. There will continue to be a split between the people on who believes what. You may not want to spend your time trying to make anyone believe anything. Just be firm in what you believe and know for yourself.

There is a tearing of the very fabric of society when these secrets become public knowledge. Those that want to hold onto the secrets may put up a fierce fight with absolute denials. We see this with people adamantly denying and often projecting their own secret actions onto someone else. We are living in a time that the more they deny, the worse it becomes for them individually. The reason for this is that we are shifting into a new world paradigm of being more true and authentic on all levels. There is no stopping this. Many of the children born on earth in the last few decades recognize and demand it.

Often, we hear the word transparency. It goes right in line with what I am speaking of. It is a call to all of us. Truth is rising, as it always eventually does. This seems to be set into motion by something much larger than us – something from the

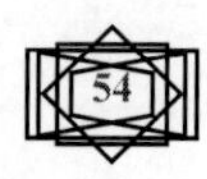

great beyond. Light is going to shine on the dark crevices. Collectively, we are all on a healing journey of some type. The only way we can walk that path is by being real and truthful – especially with ourselves. Secrets are kept for many reasons. At times, they are held onto by some to control others. We see this on a world level often. Secrets are also kept inside us because we hold shame around whatever the secret is about and we also may fear retribution.

Right now — we need to tip the scales. It is time for us to push love over fear and hate; and freedom over restriction. We must shine our light and be who we are — another light in the darkness. It is time for all of us as starseeds, empaths, and lightworkers to focus our energy, thoughts and emotions on everything good that we possibly can. In doing so, this will tip the scale of this earth.

We are all at different spiritual levels, and this is not meant to be condescending in any way. It is no different than I explained in Book I than first graders, sixth graders, seniors and college students. Some have more experience and knowledge. We cannot wait around for the first and sixth graders to understand what we know. We cannot sit around and say "Woe is me. What is happening to the world?" Instead, we must show them. We must be a shining example. We must hold that space for others. Many of you are already doing this but perhaps without the consistency that you would like to.

Many things can put us off course. Some of those include social media, radio and television news. It is so easy to get sucked in. When you participate in those things, you need to be very mindful and cognizant that it can affect you and take your energy down. It can put you in a position where you are not going to be as helpful to the world and this is what you came here for - to create, help, experience and spread joy. This is part of your purpose. Now, it is important that we regulate our emotions and that we stay in touch with our feelings. Meditation and prayer are components that give us great

results. And when we pray, we do so not in a position of asking — but in a position of affirming and seeing it done. Amen = So Be It. March on with the light and spread the love.

This is being in our power!

8 – Other Selves

"Even though you may want to move forward in your life, you may have one foot on the brakes. In order to be free, we must learn how to let go. Release the hurt. Release the fear. Refuse to entertain your old pain. The energy it takes to hang onto the past is holding you back from a new life. What is it you would let go of today?" ~ Mary Manin Morrissey

Connecting to others living in our density can be exhilarating such as when we are in love, give birth to a child, or merge with another on a deep emotional level. However, for the empath who has built inner skills or been gifted with same, connecting can sometimes be painful or disturbing. We often know when people are not being truthful with us and perhaps even with themselves. Empaths smell deceit and feel greatly impacted by it, not knowing how to navigate it very well.

For one thing, we may know deceit is occurring, but feel powerless to call it out to the individual or group involved. This is because our only proof it is happening could be our gut impressions or information we are receiving telepathically or in some other manner. It is difficult to make that your basis of proof to the other side if you choose to confront them on lies or misdeeds. It is almost like you must painfully sit back and watch events unfold that create more pain. This pain can be affecting just you or it could be affecting others. What can we do when others are deceiving and we know this but do not yet have visible, tangible concrete proof?

Step away mentally and allow things to play out. Perhaps journal your impressions of the situation, but then close the journal and let it go. Spend time generating an equal amount of true love in your immediate world to counteract the deceit you found yourself surrounded by. Play and have fun. Celebrate things that are good around you. Instead of getting caught up in the deceit drama to where it is sucking good energy from you and affecting your field, see it in your mind's eye as a cartoon that is occurring over to the side of your reality. It's not real. All is an illusion on a macro level of looking at things. Yet, in this earth space, all feels very real. It is good to keep this in mind, however, because it does give you the opportunity to step out and above things. Pretend you are at the space station, looking down at the planet you inhabit and where this situation lies. See how small it is now from the bird's eye view? Plus, you are engaged in this lesson but viewing it from a higher level on the spiral of life than you did months or years ago. You have grown in your ability to see things from a higher perspective.

Yes, there are reasons you see the deceit or become part of the untruthful situation, but your approach can now be different by easily changing your perspective. As you do so, the weight of the drama begins to lighten. You are learning to break its hold on you and that is why it is losing its grip and power over you. Things that would have nagged you for days, now turn into hours or minutes as you work out the mental logistics of it all and allow it to fade in its importance.

I have been in these same situations or similar. There are still way too many instances where I encounter people or situations such as this. I understand at a core level how difficult it can be to switch gears mentally and make the attempts to let things play out. I understand the fears one feels when they step away and let the dominoes fall. I also understand that I can never walk the path of the magical empath if I do not learn how to do this and it correlates with my own personal power and

boundaries. It is difficult and I fail at times. I forgive myself for when I am allowing it to rule over me, correct it and move on.

For the most part, relationships with others are the pinch point where these dramas are lived out. Some of these relationships can be avoided or ended. In other situations, this is more difficult to achieve. As an empath, you know that you have a tendency to attract people into your life that may suffer from negative personality disorders. This was covered quite a bit in Book I. Going no contact with some of these individuals may be the only way you can progress and live the life you desire and deserve. This is always an individual situation as each is unique. Regardless, now that you are more aware of these things and have a greater sense of your empathic nature, you are free to make better choices concerning the handling of intense conflicts or divisions between you and another.

While it may be difficult to believe, in a way that is perplexing, these individuals are in our lives to teach us something. It could be how to speak up and not swallow mistreatment to "keep the peace". The lesson may involve setting better limitations and boundaries with others. Look for the lesson you need to master. As you do so, magically these people and their dramas begin to fade into the background. Often, they disappear altogether. At rare times, something really does transform within their lives to make them different going forward. But this is very rare. Never hang your hopes on someone changing. Keep your focus on you and the internal changes you need to make to transform your outer world.

If you have difficulty knowing for sure who is good for you and who is not, ask these questions about everyone in your life from family, work and community:

- Who are the people that I can count on to understand me?
- Do I feel support from certain people and others not?

- Who are they?
- Do I feel anyone in my circle manipulates or tries to sabotage me or situations around me?
- Do I feel a power struggle with anyone?
- Do I feel someone is clouding me with their negative energy consistently?

Allow these situations that have been causing distress to fall away. Breathe in and exhale out any negativity you have accumulated throughout the experience. Let it be what it is. Truth always rises to the top. All will be revealed and your position is not to be the one who had knowledge and "knew", but to be well away from the situation when it implodes and the lies are exposed. Try not to control or even imagine the outcome as truth rises. The more you emotionally and mentally detach and allow the lives of others to play out, the more room you are making in your own body/mind/spirit experience to allow good things in. This can include inspiration, ideas and whispers from your higher self or God Source.

Spend time with others you can laugh with and have fun. This counteracts much of the negativity you experienced during any drama you were a part of. Entering a new head and heart space with all of this will assist you in removing blockages and balancing over activity in your chakras. Nature is also one of the best healers for assisting you in coming back into balance.

Try to call upon your own empathy with a sense of forgiveness toward the person(s) or situation. While this can feel daunting to take on, just give it an attempt. Can you imagine how much empathy God/Goddess/All That Is contains to forgive all of us for our transgressions? Because we have all lied and lived untruths at different points of our lives. We have all been negative and difficult. Sometimes we do not even know we are doing it. We lie to ourselves or we lie to others out of fear of some sort. This does not mean you should keep

someone around in your life that moves about in the world and engages this way repeatedly, especially without remorse, admission or real change. It just means that you drop your anger toward them replacing it with perhaps a feeling of disappointment, but forgiveness even unspoken for the way they are living their life. It is difficult, but just remember the more you stay embroiled in the situation with lower base emotions arising, the harder it is for you to fulfill your true purpose.

It is so easy when we look at others to see how they keep their good away from them in life - how things could be smoother or many things could work out so much better. Yet, it might be hard for them to see and it is the same with us. A lot of times we can see someone else's faults, how they are stuck in some sort of pattern. But we don't see it clearly for ourselves. We can clearly see how someone keeps sabotaging their life, but it is hard to see in our own.

If you have someone in your life that you are really close to, that you trust and you feel will give you the right feedback, ask them to help you see anything that is not easily revealed to you. Many times, they can be helpful in showing you what these patterns are that you may hold within yourself. In fact, you could even be sabotage partners. You could let each other know gently and clearly how you see this developing in each other's lives so that you can work on clearing it away. If you have no one to do this with that you can really trust and have a deep bond with, pray for this to be revealed to you in a gentle, but effective, way.

The larger benefit of being more particular of who is in your inner circle is obvious as you experience less stress and turmoil. When you engage in a community of people where drama is low and truth is high, it sets up a vibrational resonance for all to expand in a positive manner. Further, it opens up an invisible portal for abundance to form. The relationships formed within the tribe of people whether small

or large has the capacity to work in a synergistic manner for all. Partnering with others in a healthy way brings a greater reward than working only as an individual, which can get lonely after a time.

In families where we see great dysfunction, truths are being hidden and personal integrity suffers. The group dynamic suffers as a whole because certain elements are so ingrained. Often, some or all in the family hold fear of challenging what is wrong and not working. This can be due to a number of reasons.

First, if dealing with one or more personality disordered individuals in a family unit, it can be impossible to get them to look at how they are affecting the rest of the group. Second, fear can be involved. This can stem from individuals calling out the untruths or mistreatment and altercations arising from the personality disordered individuals. This is a very sad situation because there never seems to be a cure for what ails the family as a unit. As time goes on, the entire way of operating within the family becomes deeply ingrained. Archetypal roles with those involved are unknowingly assigned at young ages and lived out. To break this is to become one's own person and take back personal power that has been leaking.

Family is important but sometimes you have to make your own separate tribe too for support and love. When I read books where people have these large, loving families with low conflict I have a deep sense of longing for the same. It's not what I have experienced. Yet, I have to look at the larger picture from the space station. What can I learn about this so that I can make my family unit better? What can I do to not fall into traps with the older, more entrenched family unit — the one I cannot change? These are important questions.

Broken hearts are more costly than losing everything you own. We all want love and to feel valued. Appreciation is

not always forthcoming from some and direct cruelty is expressed in a number of ways that can lead to our hearts being affected. Losing a person we love and never being able to see them again can leave a vast dark chasm within us. Grief is also part of a broken heart and something that is worked through over a period of time. No amount of money or tangible assets can correct this. Hold hope even when we feel torn apart by situations with others. Take comfort as the sun rises each day, the birds wake and begin their song. Your uni-verse - your singular song is just as important and an integral part of the whole. Trauma and pain always come to some end. Have vision and know that your renewal and a rebirth lie ahead of you.

Above all, remember this empath: never dim your light or compromise your values and integrity to fit into any group or feel accepted. Hiding the true you is no different than telling a lie. Stand in the essence of who and what you are, even if others do not accept it or care. Just be you. You are as individual and unique as a fingerprint or a snowflake. Find your authenticity in situations. Keep your limitations and boundaries in place … and shine.

Notes – Thoughts – Ideas – Affirmations – Dreams

9 – Non-Physical Reality

"Mathematical science shows what is. It is the language of unseen relations between things. But to use and apply that language, we must be able fully to appreciate, to feel, to seize the unseen, the unconscious." ~ Ada Lovelace

In the past, I saw things as physical and non-physical. As I learned more about energy and the way our life experience is structured, I began to view it all as one big cosmic soup. I might be a green bean floating in the vegetable soup. Perhaps I cannot see the onions with their translucent quality in the broth beside me. Or, maybe I can only see them if one floats very close by. As a green bean, I am truly limited to what my veggie senses can pick up on. The analogy is the same for us as humans. There are animals with a greater range of hearing than we have. I believe cats see things we cannot view with human eyes. Birds, bees and other insects know when the weather is going to change long before we do. There are invisible things all around us as participants of this cosmic reality we find ourselves living in. Perhaps a better term is visible and non-visible reality.

As an empath, you have more sensory feelers out that allow you to pick up on things perhaps someone else would not notice. This can be something very local to you, extend to the planet, or even the galaxy you live in. Of late, I have experienced a couple of days where I knew something was off. It felt as if an event or events were going on that were greatly affecting the moods of those around me and myself as well. It is powerful to just acknowledge this and allow it to be. All things pass. Even if you cannot directly identify the causal factor, stepping back and just putting yourself in an observer position can assist you in working through any uncomfortable or distressed feelings. With this awareness, you can prevent miscommunication with others by letting them know, "I'm not feeling myself today. I'm sorry if I am not clear about things."

Occasionally, we have actual signs of things we need to pay attention to. Nothing is random. All events and things are connected or you would not experience it. Love has a way of pushing in front of us what we need to see, hear, learn experience, recognize or be. You are a human be-ing. You are a spirit or God like essence particle inside a miraculous biological housing that is constantly evolving and becoming.

All things come around in a circle, churning toward lessons accomplished or not. Once the circle is completed, it deviates to a spiral akin to the shape of a vortex that takes you to another level to complete yet another circle. This is a part of sacred geometry and the fabric of creation.

Evolution upward on the spiral vortex does not have to be a slow progression for those that feel impatient with processes. By diligently applying the laws of manifestation, moment by moment, day by day, you can make progress at a faster pace. However, it is important to know that any evolution would also include plenty of opportunities to hone the skill of patience. Sometimes, this is how the cosmos laughs at us. Here we are in such a hurry, yet we do need to be able to embrace the skill of patience.

We are now, however, at a precipice — a point where it would be intensely beneficial for you to choose this acceleration. Many have done so already, trying to match the speed of the current wave that has sped up in our universe. Just as a squirrel can leap to a higher tree branch, you have the capacity to make this jump by watching and listening for signs.

This is a special kind of patience where you stand ready to act, but only in response to the right stimuli. You may have experienced this in the past and know exactly what I speak of.

The clearest information I can impart regarding this leap and speedy course of self-discovery and mastery in a language is to say that you must open your sight to recognizing synchronicities — coincidences which are a way you are being shown or nudged that you need to do something. Often, it is something to help you. It can also be coming to someone else's aid.

Opening of the ears is important to hear direct thoughts, messages and communications. You may be physically blind or deaf and still able to see what is in the mind's eye or hear what is in the inner sections of your brain — the messaging system. Likewise, open your heart to experiencing your feelings of gratitude for the smallest of things. Open your solar plexus area to feel if something resonates true with you.

Another way you can progress on your path is to be inviting and open to listening to your spiritual guides. Fear is understandable with this as many do not know if they are hearing or intuiting positive entities. It is possible to connect with those onions in the cosmic soup that are toxic — just as you can with humans in this dimension. Much of this depends upon where you are resonating. If your frequency is high and mostly loving, it will be difficult for negative entities to be around your vibration.

For those so gifted and there are many of you, open your sixth chakra or third eye to receive deeper messages. Using your fifth chakra, speak your truth and honestly be who you are through the words and ideas you say. Remember the growth you experience is not to be lathered on people you come into contact with — but only revealed in small portions for them to embrace or not.

Practice not only being unselfish with others but also with yourself. Make sure to set boundaries in your dealings with others. You are not to blame self or be less of yourself (selfless). Be helpful to people in degrees. Self needs strength for the journey up the next rung into the spiral.

Our health state is a wonderful feedback system for giving us signs. All health emanates from the emotional body first and manifests itself in the physical body where it is actualized for us. It can show us where we have blockages and hurts to be healed. Something as simple as a sore throat can tell us we are not speaking up for ourselves and are holding fear in that area. Utilize your state of health as feedback to what needs correcting on other levels of yourself.

In addition to being in tune with your health and how it is manifesting, spending time in meditation is almost mandatory to live a very magical life and maintain a certain degree of calm, peace and balanced equilibrium. For those who say you cannot meditate, try this: just sit comfortably and breathe in the following manner with your eyes closed. Do this no matter what is going on in your mind. It does not matter. Just begin doing this as a calming and healthy way of connecting with your heart.

Again, make sure you are sitting comfortably. If you cannot sit, lie down and be as relaxed as you are able to be without tension in areas of the body that you are holding onto. The deep diaphragmatic breathing will also assist in ridding yourself of toxins and tension.

With eyes closed, your breathing pattern will be simple. Breathe in deeply through the nose and hold for five seconds. Blow the air out through your open mouth and if you make deep guttural sounds with the exhalation, that is ideal. This is the type of deep breathing that really moves lymph through your system and helps rid toxins. Additionally, you will feel release of tension you were holding that you were probably not

aware of. Take approximately twenty breaths in this manner. Then go about your day.

After a bit of time, you will find that you can go back to this breathing exercise and perhaps try sitting silently in a form of meditation. If your mind is filled with thoughts during your meditation quiet time, just allow them to come. Notice each thought and then let it go like a helium filled balloon. Soon, it will be easier to sit quiet through meditation without so many thoughts. As you learn to relax deeper, it is very likely the thoughts that come to you will be from a higher source. As many that have gone before have said and I believe as well, meditation is us listening to God and prayer is when we speak to God. No matter your beliefs, meditation provides a way to plug into the invisible and allow it to tell you things you are not seeing or paying attention to in your busy day to day visible reality.

Protection

Some claim that the brighter you shine, the more you attract negative entities. I disagree. Often, fear can grip you on your path as you ask yourself, "Am I vibrating at a high enough frequency to engage with my guide(s)?" This is why many rituals have been created to carve out a sacred space — a boundary that says only this exists within this perimeter and nothing else.

Despite the negative connotations with the pentagram, it is and was an original protective symbol to seal in good energy and keep out dark. Some have used it for other means for sure, but this seems to be the original intent. Indeed, just a circle made up of like-minded people or delineated in salt or some other barrier substance can be made to seal in your good intent and keep out ill will. How and why does this happen? It all has to do with the energy held within the circle. Again, when it is full of enthusiastic love and life, it repels darker

things. Like attracts like as they resonate on the same frequency.

Why do we build churches, mosques or temples? It provides a place or structure in which to connect to the divine and hold as sacred space. Circles you can make for nothing can often be more energetically powerful than a beautiful temple one may enter. I have entered some homes where I immediately know the structure is treated as a sacred space and personal temple. I have entered gardens where I feel the same. Experiencing God Source divinity can happen anywhere you desire and decide to consecrate it as so. When we make a circle to encapsulate energetic frequencies, it becomes a collective item unto itself. The circle is a culmination of thought forms emanating from the person(s) who enacted it. In other words, the power of the circle is built on thoughts and emotions. You are the power behind the creation of it and you were gifted with this ability as is told in the book of Genesis in *The Holy Bible*.

When you feel any need for protection, another method you may utilize is to simply encircle your body with a ring of light. Your body is also known as a temple. In the New *Testament of The Holy Bible* it states,

"Or do you not know that your body is a temple of the Holy Spirit within you, whom you have from God? You are not your own, for you were bought with a price. So glorify God in your body." 1 Corinthians 6:19-20

These words of the disciple, Paul, were in relation to sexual immoralities yet they pertain to all aspects of housing the Holy Spirit within each of us. There are God/Goddess/All That Is pieces of divinity within every human being. How do we honor that is the question. One way is how we treat our bodies overall. Are we not all guilty of excesses of some sort? Periodic purification can not only help be a tool of psychic self defense, it is a wise thing to indulge in as a part of self love and self care.

Have a verbal contract with your guardian angel or spirit guide(s). For instance, you could ask your guide to speak to you through symbols, synchronicities and other such things that do not seem quite as frightening to you. You could ask them not to speak to you auditory unless you were in danger or needed to know something immediately. As you begin a conscious relationship with your guide in this manner, it gives you time to discern if the symbols, nudges and advice you are receiving are beneficial or not.

So often when initiates become involved with the esoteric sciences, they have fears arise about some disincarnate entity attacking them. I have experienced these fears as well. If there are religious doctrines that have been learned, some may be kept if true and some may need to be exposed as an untruth so it can be easily unlearned. But, how do you know these answers?

Most of the time, this is an idea that has formed around fears in our mind. In our currently reality, the only people we may have to be wary of spying on us or who could be targeting us are the government and the weirdo down the street. Just kidding — sort of. Seriously, many times it is in our minds and while that may seem to give it a bit of substance, it does not mean it is really occurring.

If you were to look at my life as a balloon, I would have many polka dots upon it. Each one would represent time periods I went through when I did not honor my spiritual life and instead became embroiled only with earthly endeavors. During the time I did this, I lacked guidance on my path. Eventually, I found it and suspect that many of us go through this time in and time out period of not connecting with spirit or God Source — not even listening to our intuition. So many times, this is when we veer off course like Pinocchio and find ourselves in challenging circumstances. At other times, it can set up a very mundane existence.

Always, it is your choice. However, it is worth the effort to connect to your higher self and spirit guides. Rely on your guides by actively asking them for assistance. Pray for assistance from angels. Wear particular crystals or amulets for protection. Do whatever gives you a sense of confidence and safety. Most of all, just be aware that the invisible is around us all and real.

Some of you have the ability to connect with others that have passed on. This could be only those you have a close emotional connection to or it could be almost anyone that "comes through". Prior to your deliberate connection with them, surround yourself in white light and place protective barriers in your environment.

Over many years, techniques have been handed down to assist us in having a psychic shield of protection. The first one I will mention here involves the energetic field around the body and drawing down beneficial knowledge from the higher self. It has been called the "tower of light" by many. Essentially, you use the power of your imagination to envision a wide coverage of light around your entire body. If you are standing, you could see it as a tower from the earth to above your crown chakra. Plus you can imagine the light coming into you from above that chakra.

Another way to imagine this, especially if you are sitting or lying down, is to make an oblong egg shape of light around your entire being. If you practice this when you do not feel you need particular protection, you will benefit in two ways. First, this exercise assists with building a stronger auric field. Second, when you come across a situation where you feel you need protection, you will be practiced in slipping into this relaxing visualization with more ease.

With all of these methods, the first step is to:

1) Steady yourself and relax by taking slow deep breaths through the nose. Release each breath slowly, but fully

through the open mouth. Do this several times to calm and center yourself. You should begin to feel more relaxation in your limbs, shoulders, etcetera.

2) If possible, visualize yourself relaxing more beginning with your toes and working your way up to the top of your head, face and jaw area. You will be breathing normally during this or whatever feels best and natural to you. If it helps to continue slow, deep breathing during this relaxation phase, continue that if you like.

3) Begin visualizing a large space around you extending out at least two feet. You are going to fill that space with light. Many people find it easier to assign a color to the light initially as to better see it in their mind's eye. Try using green, blue or violet. See it completely surrounding your entire human body like a force field. Once you are imaging this well, visualize a round ball or sphere of sparkling white light floating just above the top of your head or crown chakra.

4) With the sphere remaining above you and not touching you, imagine this is a representation of your higher self. Ask it to bestow upon you any knowledge, information or beneficial vibrations you need at this time. Then wait a few seconds. In your mind's eye, see the glowing sphere begin to rotate above you swiftly at a dizzying pace. As it finally begins to slow down, see sparkling elements of light sprinkle down upon your body and aura, gifting you with what you need to know or receive.

Many cleanse and purify their environment utilizing white sage or palo santo. I do recommend this highly. Often, it is not some unknown non-physical entity we have to worry about, but rather the stale, stagnant and sometimes harmful emotional energies that can linger inside a home or a particular room. Whether tense stress happens inside that area or outright arguments, an emotional imprint can be present. Clearing the area regularly with the smoke of smudging will help. Make sure you are careful and do it correctly. White sage actually has

many anti-bacterial properties. If someone in your home has been ill, it is always good to sage the room or areas where they have been.

Having a pot of sage along with rosemary growing in your environment is always a good idea. Many also keep it growing close to the entry of their abode. These plants are fairly easy to maintain and as they begin to bloom, cut off the tops and use them in your cooking to add yummy flavor.

Utilize beautiful music to change the vibration of any area on short notice. Keep certain sound selections that you love on your phone, tablet, or music system of any type. The right music can affect your mood, taking your vibration higher. Find what works for you. Music and sounds such as drumming, chanting and other instrumental patterns have been used for centuries to help induce altered states for prayer and meditation. Music is used extensively in religious ceremonies including weddings, funerals and church services. There is a reason for this. Foster a light, joyous connection with God Source by singing your praises of gratitude. Drive the doldrums and gloominess in a room or skies away with song and praise. This is connecting in a magical way.

There are many ways to use sounds, rituals and materials from nature to change your vibration internally and around you. Often, we just forget to do these things. Sometimes, we may be feeling too loaded down with our emotions to make the first move toward feeling better. That is when we must dig deeper within ourselves and make a move toward creating a beautiful, magical atmosphere for ourselves and our lives.

10 – Energy

"Matter is Energy ... Energy is Light ... We are all Light Beings." ~ Albert Einstein

Empaths have a natural propensity to work with energy. Many serve as healers in one or more disciplines. While we tend to think of an energy healer as working with hands on healing, a vast number of ancient traditions are utilized in working with energy for healing ourselves or another. Additionally, energy may be utilized by the empath to set a special intention they want to achieve.

By immersing yourself in some sort of energy play, you will heighten your ability to have a more keen awareness of energy around you on a consistent basis. It is desirable to practice one or more of these energy disciplines as a magical empath. The reason is the same as if you were a musician … you must play and practice one instrument or more. This keeps you in your music and not feeling as if a part of you is now lost, never to return. Practicing some sort of energy discipline keeps you in your flow and magic. Let's look first at several energy healing methods and then move onto utilizing energy with ritual.

The best way to know energy is to feel it. Learning Reiki helped to reconnect me with my ability to feel the loving touch of the invisible in a large way. Reiki has been described by some as meditation that originates from the body without regulating it through mental activity as a practitioner might with various forms of trance meditation. I found that the effects were heightened for not only the recipient of the Reiki, but for myself as well by entering a trance like state where a type of loving nothingness exists as we open our body to be used as an instrument by God Source. These benefits I felt could have happened because I practiced meditation for years before embarking upon Reiki. Either way, Reiki has its own way of opening you to feeling energetic patterns that are unseen and may lead you to want to deepen your experience by going deeper with meditation separate from your Reiki. The more you practice this healing, you will find you also increase your ability to focus and feel calm inside. Reiki is an energy healing art that benefits both the giver and receiver of each session.

You may want to learn Reiki to use it upon loved ones around you and yourself. You can also expand that to others far away and even the planet as a collective. If you feel you want to make your God Source connection stronger during Reiki, I encourage you to begin a separate meditation practice which will make this happen because each discipline is complementary to one another. You will find this can be true for most energy work.

Acupressure & Acupuncture

While these healing modalities may seem mysterious, they are built upon a logical system of energy flow throughout our bodies. Just as blood flows throughout to keep tissue nourished and alive, our chi is the unseen reality life force running through us. Chi can experience blockages and over stimulation as I explained in Book I with the chakra system. Acupressure and acupuncture are based upon the same principles but with a slight difference. Through ancient medical systems, certain key areas or points have been identified throughout the human body. These areas are numerous and

interconnected with one another in a system of meridians that show the energetic flow pattern. Activation of particular points has the ability to allow chi to flow in a more measured or increased way as necessary.

Acupressure uses the pressure of fingers on those points to do so and acupuncture is very precise with thin reeds much like needles that are placed directly in the point area to balance. Both are very beneficial. In addition to possibly incorporating one or the other into your medicine chest, you may want to train to become a practitioner of same to assist others with their energy life flow. These healing methods can also bring great relief to those experiencing chronic pain, release of addictions and more.

Channeling

Empaths may become trance channelers wherein they fall into a deep meditative state and allow themselves to be the voice for another entity or group. This is not for the novice as you are in a more vulnerable psychic state during the act of channeling. It is important that you train with someone who is very experienced for guidance. Otherwise, you could possibly learn things the hard way. This is the most intensive form of channeling.

There are less mentally taxing and intrusive forms. You will know if this is something you have a natural gift for, although it can also be nurtured and learned. Again, trance channeling is accomplished almost in a semi-conscious or sleeping state. For some, the toll on physical endurance during trance can be significant as they bring forth very different vibrations through their body instrument.

Other ways things are channeled are often taken for granted. For instance, many great pieces of artwork and music have been channeled by the artist from an unknown angelic

source, higher self or what is often referred to as their muse. Numerous authors can tell you they have experienced automatic writing at times that is channeled in some way. Great inventors and scientific discoveries have come through this invisible passing of information from an unknown source to the receiver who then puts the invention or discovery into practice. Channeling is definitely a way of becoming a receiver of information. You just want to make sure it is coming from a good source and not some unseen trickster.

The ancient energy movement Tai Chi allows one to harness energy and utilize it in different ways. When one begins to learn tai chi, they master each separate step. Yet, the eventual goal of the practice is a flowing movement that is much like a dance — an energy dance. In many indigenous cultures we see a history of flow, physical movement to rhythms that move the life force around and basically stir things up … gets things flowing. Tai chi has a more graceful component to it. The movements flow from one into another and require breath work as well. It can be practiced by many people of various ages and actually can increase your energy instead of depleting it as some would think. While not strenuous, tai chi is disciplined. Adding the breathing techniques along with treating the entire experience as a meditative practice gives it even more power. Tai chi derives and is a form of qi gong (chee gung).

Qi Gong is revered by many as a discipline for adepts and those in training to be spiritually advanced. This discipline involves energy movement, meditation and breathing techniques. The movements in this practice have been described as slow and perhaps something only older adults would engage in — and many do. Ultimately, qi gong can be exquisitely slow and more difficult than it looks. Some claim the movements of qi gong help them to focus better on being intentional about things. It could assist greatly with manifesting skills. The power of focus and intention are complementary to

manifesting anything. Much of this can be accomplished by engaging the imagination while performing the movements.

Yoga is another disciplined energy movement practice that involves becoming still or meditative inside that is very beneficial. Yoga is not just an exercise to remain limber but also a spiritual practice. There are at least eleven types of yoga in existence. Practitioners enjoy improved health, less stress and increased concentration.

In summary, there are at least three main movements of energy that involve using your breath, body positions and your mind that put you in touch with your qi or life force. Each one has offshoots or branches that contain differences that may appeal to you. Moving our physical vehicles and combining it with the breath and mind focus will assist you greatly in appreciating, understanding and even manipulating life force energy.

When we work with plants, herbs, flower essences, essential oils and crystals, we further enhance our ability to feel and appreciate energy. All of these physical substances vibrate a little differently than the invisible qi we spoke of before. Nonetheless, they contain significant vibrational energy of their own. Choose one or more that speaks to you.

Thought is a very fine high vibrational frequency. Many of the disciplines above for energy work teach you to be more in command of your thoughts. Unconsciously or consciously, we have the ability to bend or change things we are currently experiencing by manipulating the energy flow and opening up fully to the life force around us. In our human frailness, we often do not see challenging catalysts as an opportunity to do this. Instead, we feel powerless and sometimes victimized by circumstances. This is where the use of rituals or even spell making can assist in pulling us out of this mind trap. To heal a situation is to bend reality. To me, it is no different than what Jesus Christ exemplified in his earthly

time. Astonishingly, he brought some back from the dead, healed others, and fed a great crowd of people with only a couple of fish. While we may not know his technique, he has told us we can do things even greater. While the majority of us feel we could not measure up to that, remember his words and do not doubt them. Much of it involves mind control that is equated with faith and belief. Some fear talk of rituals or spell making. Like everything, it only becomes evil or negative when we attempt to impose our will on others, thus denying them the freedoms they rightly deserve.

To utilize candles, crystals and other props in our wishes or spells is only to add ritualistic "um-pf" to the situation desired – to give it more physical meaning rather than being carried as a thought form only. When we look at what Dr. Dyer had mastered during his lifetime, we see that his ideas of "wishes fulfilled" is the same as spell casting. The problem is the negative images and demonization that has transpired for centuries now against those who practice this ancient root knowledge. Indeed, some have used and continue to use this birthright power to harm others or infringe upon their free will. Yet this goes on everywhere within personal relationships where manipulation, abuse or neglect exist. It also happens within religious and political systems where those who hold power or have been elected choose to affect the masses by constructing their versions of reality and rule making; thus creating life circumstances for those who are asleep to their own power.

So, as we look at spell casting, it is obvious it goes on constantly for the major prerequisite for this task is thought. These thoughts, fueled by desire and focused with intention are enough, by themselves, to bend current or future circumstances – thus changing reality of the observer and the participant.

> *"Spell referring to magic incantation is of different origin. That word is strictly Germanic (from the noun spel) and refers to talk,*

storytelling, gossip, and a sermon. It also is the derivative of gospel (which translates to "good tale") and is the source for the magical power and enchantment senses of spell." (Merriam-Webster, 2021).

> *From c. 1200 as "an utterance, something said, a statement, remark;" meaning "set of words with supposed magical or occult powers, incantation, charm" first recorded 1570s; hence any means or cause of enchantment* (Etymonline, 2021).

English poet Edmund Spenser ties those senses of the word together in his epic poem *The Faerie Queene* (1590):

> *"Spell is a kind of verse or charm, that in elder times they used often to say over everything that they would have preserved: as the night-spell for thieves, and the wood-spell. And here-hence, I think, is named the Gospel, or Word."*

> *The word gospel from "Old English godspel "glad tidings announced by Jesus; one of the four gospels," literally "good spell," from god "good" (see good (adj.)) + spel "story, message" (see spell (n.1)). A translation of Latin bona adnuntiatio, itself a translation of Greek euangelion "reward for bringing good news" (see evangel). The first element of the Old English word originally had a long "o," but it shifted under mistaken association with God, as if "God-story" (i.e. the history off Christ)."* (Etymonline, 2021).

God Source spoke our entire galaxy and more into existence. If you read the very beginning of The Holy Bible in Genesis, each element and inhabitant was placed into being by this great Creator God Source stating it — speaking it to be so.

You, as a human, have been formed in the image of this great Creator. You were given the ability to create and co-create with your God Source. The connection has been hidden for most of humanity, but it is plain as day. It is recorded in the holy books and you have many examples including that of Jesus, to see that you can create your reality and participate in being intentional about your life.

Thoughts and words have power whether you formulate a spell or not. Affirmations and prayers can be types of spells to help you eliminate negative thought patterns or reach certain things you want to achieve. The important thing is how you use your energy — for positive or negative. Each time you infringe upon the will of another, you are lessening the overall life force of all. Each time you enhance yourself and give without expecting anything in return, you expand the overall life force energy we all participate in. This has every opportunity to be a beautiful tapestry of living light we are weaving.

11 - Paths

"All journeys have secret destinations of which the traveler is unaware." ~ Martin Buber

Blindly we often travel to find our purpose in life. Time goes by and it occurs as we walk a path to an unknown destination. While we may hold overall goals for personal achievement in various life areas, ultimately we do not really know where the path will lead. As we walk, skip, run and sometimes drag ourselves along life's path, we meet up with "others" who we attract and have something to teach us if we open our spiritual eyes and ears. Those "teachers" we encounter can be embraced or rejected by us at any time. And there will be times we want to run or escape from some of the individuals or situations we encounter. This is natural and normal.

Yet, if we look the lesson in the eye and say, "Come here to me now. Show me what I need to master", we could be pleasantly surprised weeks or months later with our inner transformation. As we genuinely ask to see parts of self and what is being mirrored back to us, the answers come. Our world around us begins to reveal where we need more compassion and love. The Universal Mind begins to line situations and people up to show us.

When you run across things on your path that are not in your highest interest or even harmful, there are ways to resolve

this situation quickly. This can come to you on any level: mental, physical or spiritual. When one of these situations happens, analyze what bothers you and find a way to send true universal love to the situation or source. If you simply build walls, cut cords or provide a type of mental or physical resistance, it is more difficult to overcome. It is much more effective to love the problem or person away, setting clear preferences or boundaries as you do so. This is much more effective and you will probably never see it again.

In order to do this it will at times require a visit to our shadow side and coming face to face with our own problems. It can also mean having honest eyes on those around you and not making excuses for them. As you see all these things mirrored to you in one way or another, you realize certain truths. That information contains your "aha" moment.

In these human bodies, we are multi-faceted. We have brought much knowledge with us and it resides much of the time outside our physical body in the auric field. When we integrate the soul part of ourselves into our human body, allowing it to synergistically form a bond, our path appears lit for a change. Suddenly, we stop denying the greater aspects of our total mind/body/spirit complex.

As a young woman in her twenties, I was told that I was an adept. Incredulously, I would question, how? I knew I was screwed up at least part of the time and it was showing in all the areas I was lacking. An adept? No way. Their response was that I was just still remembering who I really was. Time showed me they were right.

I wish it had not taken so long, but I guess I made a few too many pit stops on the way as I traveled my path. These diversions all taught me things, yet they were often very hard lessons. One day, I was reading *Walking In The Light Everyday Empowerment of the Shamanic Life* by Sandra Ingerman, someone I highly respect. From the introduction of the book

alone, I realized that I have always had a shamanic persona. This is the adept side of me that had been there all along, hiding somewhere and slowly making itself known over many years. As soon as I made the realization of this, synchronicities occurred that confirmed this information.

A few days after my first book, *Dreaming Synchronicity: Journey of an Empath* was published, I was listening to a podcast and the featured guest was Dr. Stanley Krippner, a renowed psychologist and professor who was speaking of his work with shamans around the world. In addition, Stanley has a vast background in dream research and paranormal studies including some work he did for the U.S. government. Feeling like I wanted to tell him about my experiences, I sent him an email telling him about my book and asking if he would like to read it. He wrote back within minutes saying he had heard of my book and yes, he would very much like to read it. I was more than a little amazed as I wondered how he know about my book — it had just published a week or so prior and I was not well known. As a friendship emerged between us over time, I realized that Dr. Krippner has associations with people all around this planet who have similar interests and perhaps one of them mentioned my book. I have had other synchronicities occur with this gracious man that are incredible and I will share elsewhere.

Over time, I received additional confirmation of this shamanic persona. One day, my youngest daughter said to me, "Mom, I think you are a shaman." Yet, even as I typed these words in preparation for this book to make its way to you, and admitted to myself that there is a little shaman coming through me, I checked my ego at the door and said, "Hello, are you trying to spiritually flatter me or something?"

It has been my understanding that the label of shaman is something bestowed on one's self by others — not something you claim as your own. It is almost like if you pronounce yourself as being a shaman, you lose some or all of your gifts.

What frightens people and what evokes respect when we think of shamans? It is something we often refer to as power or powers — abilities the average person does not have or has not developed. We either trust the shamanic path individual to wield that power lovingly in a healing way or we do not. In that case, we fear they may do something destructive.

Today, I received another confirmation from a friend I've made over the Internet in Canada. She wrote to share a video of a woman who discovered that she was a shaman by accident. My friend suspected the same thing of me. I cannot wait to share with her the synchronicity of this as she is also one who experiences such events. She has no idea that I just began writing this chapter hours before she sent me the email.

From the time I was small and began making friends in my neighborhood, the other children called me a witch. Growing up, I felt ugly and different from the others. My closest friends did not call me this name, but others did and frequently. I thought it was my hair or teeth … something about me they thought was witchy in nature. Yet, I realized as I became older and people gravitated or were repelled by me that it was just something I unconsciously emitted.

It did not matter that I wore the same sort of clothing as others or even looked like a professional business woman, sometimes an acquaintance or someone I just met would walk up to me and say in a hushed tone, "are you a witch?" and they would give a sly smile as if I could admit such a thing to them and they would keep it a secret. I had to giggle when people did this. Genuinely wanting to know, I would ask them why they thought I might be. They could never say exactly. It was always something like, "you just have that look or feel about you" kind of thing. I never admitted to being anything but me, because I don't consider myself to be a witch.

Here is a confession that really brings home the point. In the early 80's, I was divorced and feeling a bit frisky I

suppose. I ended up taking a guy home with me that I met at a large bar that was frequented by singles. After the one night stand, I awoke with him beside me in the morning and said, "It's funny, I had a very vivid dream about a friend of a friend last night" and stated her name. You would have thought I prodded this cowboy with a branding iron. He shot up naked from the bed so quickly. Gasping he asked, "are you a witch?" Turns out, he was this girl's boyfriend. I had no idea, but my dream world did. I felt horrible, as if I had betrayed this woman I barely knew, but was innocent of that knowledge going into it. Yet, was I? Even though I had some alcohol in me, didn't I feel my intuition saying don't do this. Needless to say, he dressed in record time and shot out of there like a bat out of hell. He had that expression a young boy would have that was in trouble with mommy. I remember thinking, "maybe I am a witch and I will never do that again".

I came to know myself better as I grew older and searched my heart. While I might leave a certain impression upon people, it seems to be built upon their own beliefs and even some misconceptions. I do not see myself as a witch or a shaman. Do I walk a type of shamanic path in life? Yes, sometimes I do. Do I have things happen around me or even because of me that could be labeled as "witchy"? Probably so.

I see myself simply as a child of The Law of One and that is what I identify with most. I do not pray to multiple Gods and Goddesses, but I have no criticism or judgment on those that do. For me, I feel comfortable completely immersed in connecting with the one Infinite Creator of all. Each must find their work and path. The Law of One is predicated upon free will for all.

How do we find our path, even as we sometimes want to deny its existence within us? No matter what you do to earn a living or sustain yourself now, over time it will change. The question is: will it change toward something you want to do - a life's work that fulfills your soul? Here are steps to finding out

what that is if you are confused. These steps also include how to bring it into fruition if you know what you want.

Most likely the things you feel you came here to do that assist you on your life journey involve talents you have a natural propensity toward. When you were growing up, you may have heard others say something about you such as "he has such a natural talent for working puzzles". It could have been, "she is such a natural artist, look at her drawing." These are clues to some of what you can and will utilize to experience your calling. Your talents or natural gifts are like a little package you parachuted into this reality with. Many are skills you may have developed in another lifetime. Whether you can walk into the messiest room or office and have it organized in no time or you can engineer a new product or building, your talents are always multifaceted in some way. Spend time thinking about yours. I have many just like you but when I was growing up no one said, wow, that girl can dream. She can predict things after dreaming. To do that would mean the people around me would have to shift or adjust their personal beliefs about things beyond the ordinary physical world .... And perhaps some did. You may also have talents that others did not recognize. They can also be hidden gifts that emerge later.

I want to say something here about natural talents. Many times I have pointed out these in other people, whether teens or adults, only to have the person negate that they hold this ability naturally. I am not sure what comparison factors they hold in their minds or lack of confidence that affects them, but it makes me very sad to hear them say they are not naturally good at something when they are. Often, we may say this because we feel out of practice with the pencil, paint brush or musical instrument. And, it should be responded to that way. Thank the person giving you the complement and you may add if you wish, I would be better but I am a little out of practice. The point is do not negate your gifts. If anything, feed and

cultivate your talents for your own personal pleasure at first. Do not worry about them being a way to make money. Do not listen to voices trapped in your subconscious that say "you can't make a living like that". Instead, be in your natural gift and give it some love by using it whenever and wherever you can for yourself and others.

Learning is part of the cultivating you perform with your talents. No one is born being great at anything without rote and repetition through practice. We practice our disciplines of choosing because we find joy in it. We also learn that we do not quit and give up when it becomes difficult. If you do that, you will be the artist with many unfinished works of art; the author who has written many books half way through; and the engineer who became stuck in the middle of a problem that they are unsure of how to solve. There are pivotal points in your creativity where you must push through. Sure, it is fine to walk away for a few hours, but you must come back to it. Sometimes a little time away from the project and going out in nature reconnects you with ideas that are fed to you from "somewhere" to solve the dilemmas you feel.

Pushing through is the difference in having a finished product or not and it will demand much from you mentally. You see, you are really only wrestling with an inner beast that says this is not right; good enough; or whatever. Get on his back and ride him like a dragon of negativity. Tell him you are in charge and yes, it may not be the best but it is yours and you love that about it. Tell him you do not have to be perfect because there is absolutely nothing that is. Tell the dragon that you know you will find ways to fix what you need to fix and allow the other stuff "to be".

Life never happens the way the naysayers predict. It is full of interesting twists and turns combined with serendipitous moments. We cannot allow our beliefs to mirror the naysayer voices trapped in our subconscious from the past. We must feed our mind our own positive, life affirming messages.

Feed and water your creativity on a regular basis — as much as you can given your current schedule. Ideas will emerge and opportunities will present themselves over time. Let things develop naturally. Major leaps are made quickly. Luckily on the road you are walking — you occasionally get a lift to the next town. This can assist in making those big leaps.

Don't push things before you are ready and watch it not work out. This leads to discouragement but can still be turned into something good with the lesson it provides. Force over allowing is not the best way. Allow things to happen in their own beautiful unraveling time. There is probably a reason for it you do not see now.

Finally, continue to pay attention to your intuition. Give it the number one spot in your arsenal of what to believe or do next.

12 – Ritual & Devotion

"Rituals, anthropologists will tell us, are about transformation. The rituals we use for marriage, baptism or inaugurating a president are as elaborate as they are because we associate the ritual with a major life passage, the crossing of a critical threshold, or in other words, with transformation."
~ Abraham Verghese

Ritual has been used for centuries to mark special occasions, represent certain life passages and add meaning to strong intentions or weak wishes. Those who were designated as healers and spiritual leaders within a community of people from early earth history usually directed ritual although all would participate with a sense of devotion. Essentially, a shaman would use ritual to set up a sacred space to assist in altering consciousness. The church has long used ritual, especially the Roman Catholics and Orthodox Jewish traditions, to signify particular ceremonies and give them extra importance. The Jewish faith has many traditions of ritual to mark particular points of the year that fall in conjunction with religious time periods to observe. Likewise, Islam has daily rituals of prayer and yearly journeys to pay tribute to Mecca. All minor and major religions and spiritual pursuits contain some form of ritual.

In our civil, daily lives, there is the ritual of birthday celebrations, the wedding vows and rituals associated with it. There are holiday rituals that can include a combination of

religious significance and secular events. Christmas would be a good example of this with Santa Claus and the celebration of the birth of Jesus Christ. In the United States, Thanksgiving is a ritual of food, family and being together each fourth Thursday in November. There are numerous rituals in our daily lives we often have so normalized that we take them for granted.

Do we need rituals to be magical empaths? Probably not. I feel you can work on yourself, growing spiritually and be very much in your flow. You can direct your destiny with skills learned and intent alone. This is the way I was for a long while as I did not see much value in ritual. Over time, I saw that ritual has the capacity to be "the lift in your arch". It is a boom to your reality creation as it gives it a little more meaning and realness. One of the best things about ritual is it can make you feel more devoted to your path and devotion is highly prized. The magical empath comes to know that being devoted each day is like walking in a dreamy prayer where they know faith and love on a deeper level than before.

Devotion is the act of cleaning, decorating and nurturing your inner temple. Regular or periodic acts of ritual can assist with that. Your ritual can be anything you desire. It could begin with a breathing and yoga practice and end with lighting a candle, stating affirmations and a prayer. Perhaps you like to play light music that calms or inspires you during your devotional time. This is a great idea because instantly it helps to change the vibe in your surroundings. There are so many ways to come up with your own rituals and devotion time. Be creative and make it fun, yet meaningful. Just as you would make a toast at a table of guests you had invited, use ritual to bring forth a wondrously live experience for you.

You see, so many answers we all want are located within us. By making this devotional time for one's self, we open a little area for it to come through to our waking consciousness. Many times, we get lucky and alter our

consciousness, slipping out of that overly analytical side and into our more receptive, creative one. At that time, giant insights and beautiful emotions may occur. Devotional time is reconnecting with our soul. As we do so with the assistance of rituals we choose, it becomes a more solemn experience than just trying to do so on the fly in the middle of the day or in a vehicle or something.

If you have potential life changes going on such as a move, career change, loss of relationship or issues with family, planned ritual and devotion practice can help keep you in balance and show you what decisions would bring you the better outcomes. Formal ceremonies marking life events provide a layer of dedication, focus and commitment moving forward with goals. Sometimes, ceremony is used for remembrance.

Finally, one of the strongest aspects of ritual and devotion is that this is a loving gift you are bestowing upon your complete body/mind/spirit complex. It shows a high degree of care about one's self. This is the self care principle that is spoken of so much. It is not just about bubble baths or massages — although those are great rituals too. The self care you display with devotional experiences is like massaging your connection to God/Goddess/All That Is. As you strengthen that, you will find things begin to shift for you in every area of your life, especially relationships. It will no longer be acceptable to you to be in the presence of people who act in certain ways. Loving devotional time changes you and for the better, helping you step into being the magical empath.

Opening The Heart

Part of the work we do that is necessary to graduate or move into the next density is activating and opening the heart chakra. There are several reasons why this particular point is relevant. First, we are moving into fourth density (fifth

dimension). Second, the heart chakra is the fourth major body chakra and it serves as a bridge between the upper and lower chakras.

Physically, your heart is a mighty muscular organ that pumps your blood to your lungs, brain, through your entire vascular system and organs. It then brings it back yet again in an amazing cycle.

Mentally, the heart represents passion, compassion, strength of force and rhythm of life.

Metaphysically, your blood represents life force and some call it joy flowing through you and nurturing every part of your body so you are sustained for the journey. When blood glucose levels are out of sync, you experience low or high blood sugar levels. Something is affecting your joy of being. Once identified, a remedy must be found.

Your heart is not a mindless mechanical pump. The tissue holds memories embedded at the cellular and even holographic level. There are many instances now recorded of heart transplant recipients taking on the personality quirks and the likes or dislikes of their donor.

In our culture, we have many sayings that involve the heart such as,

"Put your heart into it."

"Straight from the heart."

"Think with your head, not your heart."

"Not for the faint of heart".

"A broken heart."

The heart has a reciprocating action. It takes in and gives out. If this balance is interrupted in some way, then the entire body system is affected. We all know of people who give and give, yet have a difficult time receiving. Many empaths are like that. We know of those who take and take, but have difficulty giving. This is a heart chakra out of balance and when this happens, the individual cannot experience things to the fullest.

The first emotion associated with our heart is love — a powerful emotion that has the ability to transform you and your world. The heart also rules the emotions of forgiveness, empathy and compassion.

While we attribute the color red and shades of pink with hearts, green is the color of this chakra. This is the color of the energy vibration we are moving into now. On the vibratory sound or musical scale, primary green correlates with the fourth major chord. It also resonates with the note "A". Remember that green is the fourth color in a rainbow. There are many associations between refracted light (color) and sound because they are energetic vibrations.

If we listen to the teachings of Jesus Christ, all that he taught is heart centered. They are fourth chakra teachings such as the concepts of forgiveness of self and others; loving your enemies instead of holding animosity or hate inside; giving to others that are less fortunate; healing self and others; treating others the way you want to be treated. These are all principles of naturally moving into this great fourth density. You will do this not out of a sense of duty, but out of a sense of joy in doing it and love mixed sometimes with empathy and compassion.

Yet, you will practice an equal amount of receiving. Remember the reciprocal action of your heart. You will take in joy and feel bliss. You will have others forgive you and accept that forgiveness. You will experience being loved and cared for instead of always being the one to do the loving and caring for. You will receive the compassion needed and feel it as a new starting point for yourself.

This reciprocal action is important for a balanced fourth chakra and moving you into fourth density higher consciousness.

I heard someone say once that the way you receive gifts correlates with the way you receive life. Thereafter, when I gave gifts to people, I would watch their reactions to receiving. I was not doing this in a judgmental way but more out of curiosity and an unscientific experimentation. Some were very grateful, one almost rejected gifts each time, saying they did not need it or I should not have done that. Another never even acknowledged they received the gift I had sent to them. I would then look at their personalities to see if these reactions demonstrated this idea. You may try this experiment on your own, also noticing your own reactions when you receive gifts.

Being grateful and feeling gratitude fuels the joy (blood) flowing through your heart. Believe it or not, even in the darkest of places, there is always the good and something you can feel grateful for. It can be so hard to see at times, but it is always there. Be gentle with yourself when you are going through turbulent times. Always, our heart is involved.

While we often think and refer to this fourth chakra as the heart chakra, it also rules the lungs, pericardium, upper back and ribs; inner arms and hands. So, we not only have the heart pumping action involved in this system, but the respiration system and immunity responses. From a physical stance, we see that a weak immune response, breathing issues, circulatory or heart disease, hypertension — all of these can indicate dysfunction in the fourth chakra.

On a psychological or emotional level, those issues may correlate with excesses and deficiencies. Excesses would show up as codependent behaviors like over caring and giving too much especially to the detriment of self. We see this often as the door mat syndrome because boundaries are not put in place. The fear behind this behavior is that you won't be loved or

needed should you institute boundaries or stop your excessive giving. Trying to be a pleaser falls into this aspect. Pleasing everyone and not pleasing self or allowing others to please you shows lack of boundaries and fear of rejection. This often leads to the martyr attitude. Here I am doing all of this for you and I get little thanks (love) in return.

If you are restricted or deficient in your fourth chakra, your symptoms could include being overly critical of people, situations, and things around you. The glass is almost always half empty instead of half full. You actually feel powerless due to the shutting down and closing off of your center chakra. There is a part of you that wants to breathe in the beauty of so many things. However, you cannot see a way to change and transform your outlook through compassion, understanding, love and gratitude. You often fear true intimacy and making yourself vulnerable.

Some may manifest the restriction in this area by withdrawn types of behavior or even being anti-social. Ultimately, by shutting down, these individuals feel lonely, isolated, cut off from their true selves and others. While you hear these words, images of others you know who display these attributes some or all of the time may appear. Acknowledge that, but let it go. It is more beneficial to apply this to self and see which qualities you may be adhering to without really knowing it. Ultimately, you have your personal power to change you, but not others — no matter how magically inclined you are. True transformation is lasting and not temporary for immediate results.

The paradox is this: we are all encapsulated in The One. We are all moving closer to reunion with the one Creator God. What we see in others is a reflection to check and see if we have this in ourselves or often, its opposite. We are in the one — the one is in us — but we are not The One — yet collectively we are the One.

How can we grow gracefully in our physical bodies and mind/spirit toward this fourth density and improved fourth chakra harmony? We return to being peaceful and centered by experiencing and showing love, compassion, empathy, being accepting of others and loving ourselves. Remember that gratitude is the magical charge that really accentuates this.

Be forgiving of yourself and others. If they or you were doing it all perfect, chances are very good they would already be in fourth density. This is because you naturally will be where you resonate. So, we are all here on earth learning to move with the planet into this new dimension created by our Creator. To make the move, we do not have to be perfect with love, compassion, understanding, forgiveness, and taking those same attributes in. Yet, there is an unknown mark or cut-off - a percentage of the time or way you conduct yourself to be eligible. In other words, you don't have to be a straight a student, make the dean's list, but you must be over a certain level to move on. This level or demarcation is unknown to me, only God knows our true essence — hearts.

So when you encounter situations or others that try your level of empathy, love, forgiveness or understanding, know that a challenge has been presented for you to overcome. Likewise, if you find yourself falling into being a martyr or giving/caring too much, your challenge is to learn a new level of self care and love; forgiveness of self; receiving instead of giving so much. Set boundary lines in a loving way to keep this new promise to yourself. If the others you have overly catered to withdraw, do not fear this. You never had their love then, did you? You just created a dependency and really a parasitic relationship where they take and you become drained.

Remember that your heart and lungs are organs that work off equal receiving and giving. They are reciprocal individually and to each other when working correctly. Keep this balance in mind as you carve out your life and you will experience peace. If you struggle with love relationships, check

out my book, *Real Love ~ Finding "The One" Lasting Relationship.*

Notes – Thoughts – Ideas – Affirmations – Dreams

13 - Rebirthing

"A rebirth out of spiritual adversity causes us to become new creatures." ~ James E. Faust

Everything is born out of desire. The frequency vibration of a newly launched desire carries a pure tone of expansion. It is not thinking of what can go wrong or what can go right. In this initial state, desire can feel as if it is outside many of the laws of the dimension we reside in. It has not been mucked up with the negative vibrations we so often encounter.

Once desire enters and germinates, it takes on the characteristics of its host. How the flower eventually blooms is conditional upon the elements it finds itself within. This is why esoteric and other philosophies encourage us to manage and cultivate love and positive thoughts.

Often, we must make changes in our environment to bring forth the best beauty of our desires. From our living spaces to the people and things that surround us, sometimes we need to let go of someone or something. This could also be a letting go of parts of ourselves that do not serve us well. By deeply knowing ourselves – those parts of us that are negative, constrictive, filled with fear or hatred, we can transmute. It is within our own transformation and resurrection that we express the divine intention that originally fueled the desire in our conception.

If we are allowing another person to squash our original expression of intention and desire, we must adjust the barriers between us and those who hinder our progress to be all that we can be. We cannot tolerate the company of those who want to mold our desire to their ideas – who only accept us if we bloom into what their beliefs and ideas say is acceptable or proper. For what we surround ourselves with is our growing medium. This is the soil providing the nutrients to fuel our dreams. If poison is contained within the ground, we will struggle to develop and always be held back.

Many humans feel a pull inside, nudging them there is something they are here on the planet to do or accomplish. Some have identified all or part of it and others have it temporarily obscured from their view. I believe we are born out of desire and not just looking at it from the sexual component. Rather, we were pure thought, fueled by intentions that sped from a photonic source. This tiny seed held enough desire to be the one to germinate, the one that got lucky and manifested into human. And you merged with like elements in order to grow into the human you are today.

When you feel the pull of "what you are here for", you are touching the outer seed surface of the original desire that created you to begin with. As you dive deep and know yourself, the desire unfolds and reveals itself to you in layers. With impatience to reveal what desire holds, you learn that trying to force it only brings frustration. Likewise, you learn that as you slow down your analytical thoughts and connect with Source through meditation, desire begins peeking out at you and showing up through intuition, impulses and synchronicities.

As we move through this third dimensional reality, veiled in most respects, it can be difficult to find that original spark of desire. We want to open the package and see what is inside. There are layers upon layers of tissue paper covering up the tiny seed that lies at the bottom. All of those layers of

wispy paper represent the ideas and beliefs you have allowed to cover the true desirous you.

To accomplish your original desire, you must be in alignment with your true being at least some of the time. If you find yourself close to this, but not there because your environment of family, work or even the part of the world you live in is holding you back, you can change this. You have control over it. Sometimes, in order to bloom bigger, we must remove ourselves from situations or people that we have let hinder our growth and keep us from expressing our original desire. Perhaps we have allowed it from our own misguided ideas of tolerance and consensus beliefs we have adopted.

Most prisons are made in our minds and are self-imposed. The locks, chains and bars holding us in are because we are not allowing ourselves to be the most we can be out of fear of judgment or failure. As we go within and seek to be on the path of desire once again, let us not hastily blame others. Yet, let us also not allow anyone or anything to stand in our way. So much of the untruths we collect in our minds and wear as an invisible cloak throughout our lives are dimming the light inside of us that desires to be refueled and shine brightly. Re-birthing can truly assist with washing away many of those thought forms keeping us small. As expansive beings at a soul level, we are meant to be as big as our desire is inside when it has not been covered over with all the mud that is so easy to collect.

Rebirth and renewal are part of the cycle — the spinning vortex of life that cranks out the seasons for all time. Each fresh beginning that emulates spring brings hope of new, better experiences and beauty. We are always incubating our seed of consciousness for this time. Nothing is ever lost, but continues changing form. Everything can undergo renewal and rebirth.

Your mind/body/spirit complex is ever changing in this realm. Each of us undergoes various degrees of periodic transformation in our thoughts (mind) and body as we age and progress along our path in life. Ultimately, this also affects the spirit as it grows in knowing itself more intimately and expands in various ways. Here is a poem I wrote in a journal many years ago:

I knew an enlightened woman once

She gave me a bright pink plastic Easter egg.

Inside were two pink candy kisses and a message that read:

"Dear, I Am, I say, who are you today?

Today you are not who you were yesterday,

And tomorrow you will not be who you are today.

So, dear, I Am, I say, just who are you anyway?"

I threw away that egg but kept the message just the same.

Later as it tossed around in my brain, I realized why that message came.

I cannot be all things to you and I cannot be all things to me.

I Am, Dear – only me.

I Am, Dear, whatever you are willing to see. (April, 1984)

How others perceive you is one thing and not something to concern one's self with. How we see ourselves holds much more importance. Our self changes with time, even for those not on a spiritual path. Our mind learns and unlearns things. We go through many experiences that can affect us on all three levels: body, mind and spirit. At times, we may feel as if we are living out a certain role, only to see that switch and transform to something else as we age. A simplified version of this would be the maiden, mother, crone phases in some neo-pagan circles.

Archetypes, however, are all around us. In my studies of the Ra Material and subsequent meditation with those channeling Q'uo, Hatonn and Lakawei, it had been brought forth that the tarot was originally created on Venus by the Ra collective entity and later brought to Egypt. On Venus, the tarot archetypes were used as thought forms passed to those seeking spiritual advancement. They were not contained within playing cards or presented to a seeker in drawings as we see today. Further, they only consisted of the major arcana cards and were not used for divination. Rather, the archetypes were a match point of contemplation for the experiencer. My understanding is they were or could be phases of one's journey through spiritual advancement (The Ra Material, 1982).

These archetypes were mental in nature and used to enhance a person's journey and experience. From my interpretation of Ra, they were somewhat subjective to each individual who contemplated the archetype. The archetypes could be separated into three groups of sevens to represent the different aspects of an entity. For instance, archetypes one through seven represent the mind; eight through fourteen represent the body or physicality; and fifteen through twenty-one, the spirit. Now, this leaves the zero archetype, The Fool. My impression is that this is the beginning archetype of any seeker who is new on their journey and ready to have a spiritual adventure.

No matter where these archetypes come from in the tarot deck, it would be interesting to trace when and how you have moved through these aspects of yourself in relation to your mind/body/spirit complex. Literature is full of additional archetypes, some more of a worldly nature and others throughout history very spiritual. Many names come to mind for me as I think of some of the archetypes one could emulate for a phase in their spiritual development such as: Dr. Martin Luther King, Ghandi, the Buddha, Jesus Christ, and more.

Rebirth can occur at each phase when an individual feels they have mastered one level or archetype and desire to try something else for their advancement. Some may even want to adopt different outer physical things to accompany this new archetype. For instance, they may wear different clothing or even adopt a new name or nickname. Rebirthing is a new commitment to a new you that has undergone some sort of change, transformation or intense learning. It can also be part of a new dedication of one's self to a goal.

Baptism in the river of Jordan was a physical representation of rebirth. This symbolic ritual was and still is a cleansing away of the old and arising from the spiritual waters into the new. The element of water has often been linked to spirituality. Water has the ability to cleanse and wash away the old. As soft as water is, running consistently it has the power to carve rock. It is a carrier and conductor. It is vital to our physical lives. And so it is with our spiritual selves.

Following the principle of the ritual and devotion, rebirth is an act of self love. It is wise to always remember that our capacity to love others is only limited by our capacity to love our self. When we approach our spirit with appreciation, forgiveness and love, we expand our growth to offer that to many. Starting new on your journey toward a washed clean, re-birthed self can be one of the deepest treasures you gift yourself. It physically demonstrates a method of washing away or letting go of the old that does not serve you. As you have

grown in all facets, the metaphorical dead layers of skin you carry no longer serve you. In fact, they could be a covering that holds you back. Rebirthing is a shedding of those layers and shaking off any debris that has collected upon you internally. It is effective as a tool to accompany any healing you are in need of.

Our universe shows us each day and night that rebirth is a natural experience to take things that are old, worn out and possibly even full of pain from the past and transform them. From changes that happen in land masses to stars that die out only to be replaced with a new one, our world reflects this principle on all levels of existence. Look at plants and the regenerative properties — especially those stubborn weeds. Just kidding, weeds are actually beneficial. Everything is when looked at through the correct lens.

The process of rebirthing one's self is intimate and special. It is an act that incorporates all aspects: spiritual, mental, emotional and physical. Rebirthing can be done at any time but should not be approached in a frivolous manner. It represents a reconnection and re-dedication to a soul's journey and growth. It can also represent moving about in this physical world with a better temperament, attitudes and more loving ways to self and others. It is almost always accomplished by an actual ceremony alone or with like-minded people.

It is beneficial to use a water source for a rebirthing ceremony in which you can connect deeply with yourself and find a sense of renewed energy. This could be utilized with a bathtub, pool, lake or ocean. The watery womb helped carry you into this world and remains a place — even in your mind — to carry you into a newly birthed you.

Some people like to fast prior to conducting any ceremony for rebirthing. There are others that may want to prepare a delicious meal to enjoy before or afterward. There are no rules with this. In fact, the more individualized you can

make your rebirthing experience, the more effective it will be. Below is a sample of how a rebirthing may be conducted. Use it as a guide to write your own experience. Journal how you feel prior to the rebirthing ceremony and for a few days afterward.

Where you see a blank in these sample rebirth ceremonies, substitute the name of the person, thing or situation you are moving away from, even if it is your "old self". Likewise, fill the blank in for what you want to manifest and attract with the new you.

Say the words slowly and with emotional meaning. Again, I want to emphasize that your ceremony will hold more meaning and resilience by crafting your own words.

Symbolic items you may want to gather for your ceremony can include a seed and new soil, plus water for nurturance.

Rebirth Ceremony

Great Creator – God/Goddess/All That Is

Thank you for this blessed opportunity to grow and be reborn again in you light and love. As I leave old things behind that no longer serve me, I call them out and ask you to assist in helping me to grow beyond those old ways.

Goodbye _________

Goodbye _________

I now embrace the new me that has left the cocoon of darkness and limited movement. I am free to wash away all residue from the past, emerging from the water a clean vessel to be filled with love, light and gratitude for all around me.

I place my desires in the hands of the Great Creator to show me their physical existence in the perfect time/space sequence for my enjoyment, sustenance and soul's journey.

My grateful heart feels love and my mind is open to brilliant inspiration. I trust that all is well in my world.

Perhaps you have a negative situation you have moved from and want to use a rebirthing ceremony to signify the new you that has emerged through this challenging experience.

Rebirth Ceremony For Removal of Negative Relationship

____________________, you have stormed and flooded my ambitions with your disapproval, criticism and fears. You have come at me like a tornado ripping away my leaves and leaving me cold, feeling like not enough. You have detached and left me thirsty for even a droplet of love when I failed to be what you believe I should be. Yet, I know that by staying in your garden – in your presence – I am allowing myself to never reach my full potential of desire.

I cannot waste moments of worry as to whether this affects you. My focus must be on giving up and going toward my original desire and intention. You will fulfill your desire as you choose and I must do the same. I wish you well.

I have uncovered the seed – the one that contains the original blueprint of my desire. I allow the winds of Source to transport this seed of desire into a beautiful, thriving patch of soil, free from fear and self loathing. I am joyous with the hope contained within, feeling the warm sun as I emerge from this embryonic darkness. I am new, original, immune and strong – stronger than ever because of the knowledge I now carry with me. I am reborn and claim my right of desire – my strength and energy drawn from God/Goddess/All That Is.

I have rebirthed myself after a long, dark journey and I now live in the sun. Cutting this final tie between us, I am free --- free to be the new me.

I feel energy and excitement as I allow the old me to wither and dissolve. I know I am fully alive in this newly sprouted seed. Allow me to open my eyes to the sun and the opportunities it brings me for growth. Allow me to capture inspirational ideas on the wind and nurture them as they come true. My heart is filled with enthusiasm. I trust my path ahead.

A rebirthing ceremony may be to your advantage when you begin a new career path or another milestone in your life such as becoming a parent. Again, I encourage you to write your own ceremony as surely as you would your own wedding vows. The more individualized this is to your circumstance, the better!

14 – Empath Specialties

"When I stand before God at the end of my life, I would hope that I would not have a single bit of talent left, and could say, 'I used everything you gave." ~ Erma Bombeck

At some point in time, someone began categorizing empaths. At times, it seems a bit forced to gain clicks or readership. Most empaths I have the pleasure of knowing hold many of the following attributes. It would be difficult to place them into one or even two of these categories. I will briefly cover these emerging types of empaths just for the sake of feeling as if I, the author, have not left anything out.

Intuitive Empath

The empath with high intuitive abilities is actually fairly common. While there may be some empaths who only feel the vibes coming from the earth or animals, intuition is generally scattered throughout all empath types. The issue is that some do not recognize it or negate it in some way. Below are ways you can hinder your intuitive abilities:

- Preconceptions of what your psychic experience would/should be like. For instance, you may be clairvoyant but not recognizing it as such. It could be

that in your mind, you believe that a clairvoyant should see things unfold in front of her or him like a high def movie. There are many ways that a clairvoyant sees. Sometimes, it is no more than a flash of an image. It could be a person, object, or place that is a little more prolonged. This vision could take place as a hazy (think misty) thing or something very clear to them physically in front of them. Many times, it is what they see in their "mind's eye". The same could be said for clairaudience and clairsentience. When I have experienced clairaudience, I have heard words in my head and also heard them aloud a few times with my ears from an unknown source. They are always wise words and the right advice if followed. Clairsentience is walking into a room and feeling as if someone just had a huge fight there even though there is no one present. It can be many feelings you pick up on things around you.

- You can actually hinder your skills at times by being too self assured. Stay humble. Spirit is much more eloquent than we are, especially when we get our ego involved. Be open to learning and new ways of doing things. You came into this open minded – stay that way.
- Lack of trust in the fact that you're receiving information. Trust that you are intuitive.
- Perfectionism – you will not be a perfect guru, psychic, wise person. You are human. Again, stay humble and be the vessel to come through. The information is probably always accurate but your perception of it may be skewed as you relate it to yourself or another.
- Allowing – free yourself from needing to be in control. Allow spirit to show you what they need to show you.

In addition, there are many specialty areas of sixth sensory living that particular empaths may be endowed with. All of them vary slightly and it is common to see an intuitive or psychic empath have several of these abilities which can

include: clairvoyance, psychometry, telepathy, clairaudience, clairsentience, claircognizant, precognition and mediumship.

Emotional Empath

Recently, the term "emotional empath" was coined to explain people who may battle feelings that have no clear explanation. It has also been purported that many with these high empathy levels find themselves in professions where they assist others directly with their life problems such as a therapist or in another career area of health. I wonder if that is actually the wisest choice? It is certain they can give their patients wonderful service, but how much baggage could they be carrying with them that could be impacting their internal feelings and their regular relationships?

One of the things we are attempting to move toward as a magical empath is leaving behind the direct taking on of other people's emotions where it is not conducive to us. This is a skill to build where you allow in what you want and do not allow in what you would rather see fly in the other direction. All of this is achievable with techniques that are real or instituted in the imagination — many of which were in Book I. Regulation also involves limitations or boundaries we initiate and enforce with specific consequences. Our ability, as empaths, is to empathize, care, love and help transform without totally giving up of ourselves. That would make us victims instead of victorious helpers.

Dreaming Empath

After I released my book, *Dreaming Synchronicity - Journey of an Empath*, I had others contact me that were also dreaming empaths. I never knew dreaming empaths prior and I tend to think there could be more of us than we realize. Dreaming empaths often travel into the unseen realms easily and pick up information they would otherwise be unable to know in their current day to day life. This could be important things about themselves, family members or friends. It could also involve local, national or world events. All of these dreams would be precognitive and pronounced with the empath. In other words, they know the dream is not just a regular "busy" one. Instead it has an emotional impact of some sort and has significance that they must decipher and determine.

Many of the precognitive dreams can be experienced in symbols. If you believe you may be experiencing empathic dreams, try first deciphering your dream based upon the emotions surrounding it. Then look at the symbols and what they mean explicitly to you. You may use a book of dream symbols if you like to help you determine the dream's message, but most of the time I have found this does not match up well for me. Experiment and find your way with this because everyone is different.

It is very important that dreaming empaths keep a record of their dreams. Often, you will see something in the future that lines up with a dream you wrote down in the past. Synchronicities can occur around the dream as well. Check out my journal I designed specifically for this on my website.

Earth Empath

This trait many empaths possess involves being most comfortable in nature. Indeed many of these empaths go out of their way to live in a very natural environment. If they are city dwellers due to other circumstances, their downtime from work will find them heading for a place in a more natural setting such as a lake, ocean, river or forest.

Earth empaths have a need to connect in some way with nature and stay grounded by doing so. These people may work

in a profession that brings them into utilizing their empathy to help the environment in some way. Some earth empaths may develop headaches or body aches when an earthquake is going to occur. An earth empath may just experience very sad feelings prior to an event or during and not know why until they finally hear about the natural disaster. Some may have precognitive dreams about these events.

Environmental (Geomantic) Empath

Some empaths have a unique talent for identifying particular lay lines within the earth. They may yield a divining rod with confidence to find a source of water. Regardless, this empathic trait allows the empath to be drawn to certain areas or feel the invisible existence of something in a particular area. Indeed, there are numerous places on our planet where unexplained energy events occur. Empaths with this propensity for identifying and finding them can be quite helpful to others.

Plant Kingdom Empaths

Many of the earth empaths overlap into this category as well. Plants and the beautiful vibrations they offer to us are essential to an empath who could be categorized this way. These individuals sometimes verbalize to the plants they care for just as they would children they are raising. These people often have a way with plants that some have referred to as a "green thumb". They gain a sense of grounding and joy from working with the plant kingdom that is not comparable to anything else in their life.

Many of these individuals have obsessions with particular flowers and could even be in the florist industry. More often, we find them having their own gardens and thoroughly enjoying working outdoors with plants. Some begin to specialize in flower essences and medicinal herbs, making

their own oils, vinegars, tinctures and creams from their bounty.

Heyoka Empath

Did you have a sibling, aunt or uncle who tried to humor another family member when they were pouting or sad? Perhaps, you try to make others feel the opposite of what they are currently experiencing. If so, this is typical of the Heyoka empath. The root of the word Heyoka most definitely originates with the Native American people. The exact tribal region is hypothesized as being from the Great Northern Plains where the Lakota and Dakota tribes were prevalent.

What stands out the most about this type of empath is they use a mirroring technique, often in a humorous way, to show others another side of things. Intuitively, it is like the Heyoka is aiming for a balancing of feelings within another person or group. Basically, when an empath is operating as a Heyoka, they feel intensely uncomfortable with the current vibe and are aiming to change it. For instance, the Heyoka may do something completely backwards in front of another to make a point. This would often be accomplished in a comical fashion.

Certainly, those that tend toward a satirical personality could have this Heyoka label. This empath personality type can also be combined with someone who is sensitive to plants or animals — or any number of combinations. Rather than categorize someone as solely Heyoka, this is a trait that may appear at various times when this empathic type personality feels the need to show others another side of things and try to achieve emotional balance.

Animal Empath

Just as the name implies, these empaths have a special connection with animals over humans. While we might not always see them working directly with animals as a vocation, these people have to be around animals in some fashion and as often as possible. Even if they live in a place where they are not allowed pets, they will invest in fish or a reptile. They may volunteer in their spare time at an animal shelter or on a horse farm. They will always find a way to get close to earth's creatures.

At a distance and close up, I have watched animal empaths do the most amazing things. One I knew simply walked into a pet store and had what was an otherwise cranky macaw take to him. The bird instantly flew onto his shoulder and walked a bit down his arm. He made noises and spoke to it and the bird seemed to love it. These people can have a natural empathic way with animals that is both admirable and enviable.

Multipotentialite Empath

A new term to describe empaths who have multiple skills is the multipotentialite empath. It is also believed that they will walk multiple paths in life and have two or more purposes they came to accomplish.

Some of the traits this individual will display include being a bit of a brainiac. They constantly want to learn and do not like allowing their mind to be idle. Many of them are on an almost constant self-improvement course of some type, whether following someone whose advice they trust or fashioning their own.

Activity of some type rules these individuals. They must be constantly creating, either in their mind in a creative way or in activities they pursue. All of this busyness can make it hard for them to slow down at times, but they seem to thrive off of their own activities they want to engage in.

When they find a job has served its purpose and now become unfulfilling, they move toward their next career path. Sometimes this move is well planned and other times not. Yet, they seem to intuitively move through life and always land where they feel they need to be and can offer the most.

Like many empaths, they often feel like they are not meant to be in this world. Yet as they age and look back on accomplishments and life lessons, they see how it was all perfect for their growth.

Dark Empath

I am not sure when the concept of the dark empath personality disorder was born, but it appears to have originated from psychological research in the United Kingdom. These studies were tied to the dark triad of personalities namely:

Narcissist Personality Disorder

Machiavellianism

Psychopathy

All three of those disorders share one thing in common, they have little to no ability to feel empathy toward others. As an empath, I know you may be very familiar with one or more of these personality types. It is unfortunate that we sometimes unknowingly attract these individuals.

Comparing the three, the psychopath is probably the most dangerous. Surprisingly, psychopathy is not listed in the current DSM V as a personality disorder. Anti-social personality disorder closely resembles it. The danger with these

individuals is no empathy for actions along with no remorse (Psychology Today, n.d.).

Likewise, the Machiavellian individual is also not listed as a personality disorder. These people are master manipulators and will do anything to make things go the way they want them. They could be very adept at seeming as if they are empathetic from watching others and learning the responses they believe they should have.

The narcissist carries extreme aggrandizement of self and truly believes they are superior to others. This personality type often uses learned empathy in order to manipulate people around them. In reality, they are incapable of really understanding the feelings and needs of others on a true empathic level.

If I were to create a dark empath character for a novel, I would choose someone who had one of the personality traits above and had built a large spiritual following. On the exterior and to many followers, everything is beautiful and seems righteous. In the meantime, people are getting hurt by this individual in a myriad of ways and are potentially gaslighted, cruelly threatened or even killed to not reveal the dark person's dealings.

The so called "dark empath" that is being labeled today is someone who has one of those personalities from the dark triad and also has high empathy. It is really important to differentiate and know that this empathy is cognitive or learned — not affective empathy which is where you actually feel what others are feeling.

Many of these dark or false empaths study people from childhood on, watching how they handle things emotionally. They also may spend an inordinate amount of time watching dramatic movies to get a sense of what people do when others are experiencing some type of emotion around something.

Somehow, a new category of empath has been created — one in which they have one of those three personality disorders plus have empathy, even if it is cognitive at its source and not naturally felt.

To me, this negates the entire aspect of being a true empath. Empaths do feel the emotions, moods and vibes of people, animals and other things around them. They have to work not to take it on themselves. An individual who has learned what empathy should look like and when it should be applied is nothing more than participating in being manipulative, like a con artist. This is very common with those affected by narcissistic personality disorder. They can act like they have empathy when they really do not. Overall, I believe a better representation of this personality type would be the False Empath, which more fully represents what is going on.

How can one know if they are dealing with such a personality? It can be difficult, but here are some signs to watch for:

Does the individual seem to secretly revel in making others jealous or angry?

Do they like to say things to push the buttons of others and then laugh or criticize the other for becoming angry?

Look at how they relate to others - are they a taker or giver. Generally, these people take more than give. When they do give a little, they will try to make others think they are the greatest person in the world for their giving.

Are they condescending toward others?

Do they make others the butt of jokes?

Overall, it is always important to pay more attention to what an individual does than what they say. Promises are great, but only if kept. Actions are the real deal.

15 – Sex & The Empath

"Sexual energy is just that, it's energy. And where we choose to expend that energy makes all the difference in the world."
~ Joy McMillan

The level of pleasure and broadness of each sexual encounter is dependent upon many things for empaths. Where they are currently resonating emotionally is important. If they are in feeling/thinking mind and lost in their upper chakras, it will not be quite as mind blowing. If they are clearer and can integrate all of their chakras into the experience, they have the real potential to enjoy tremendous sensations on the physical, mental emotional and auric fields of their mind/body/spirit complex.

All of this can happen either spontaneously or in a measured, planned way. With empaths being very giving plus responsive to what their partner is feeling, this reciprocal partner can indulge in a type of encounter that is above the fray compared to others. The empath's need to please is high, yet the act must be reciprocal in points of pleasing one another to take it to a higher level. Two coming together should not be one sided in the level of pleasing each other.

Ultimately, there are many elements that heighten sexual encounters to lofty clouds where you envision, hear and feel the fireworks explode. There is knowing exactly what heats you up and eventually brings you over the edge.

Atmosphere and environment can play a huge part. Role playing can add new excitement in a long relationship or marriage. Use of certain scents, tools, and fantasy can add a newness to each encounter. Indeed, having an imagination about how you encounter one another makes for a sublime experience as long as each can agree on the manner and methods.

Many people are taught, often from infancy, that it is bad to touch ourselves in the genital area. These messages from parents are misguided, but well meaning. They can become deeply ingrained in our subconscious. When this has occurred, we will often put off touching our bodies in those areas or at the very least, not engage with our bodies in a self fulfillment exploratory way. For others, the act of pleasing one's self holds no guilt or shame and it can assist greatly in leading a more beneficial experience with a partner. If you do not know that lightly touching your left inner thigh makes you feel in the mood … or that even someone lightly stroking your cheek has this same effect upon you, you will be missing out on great sex that is not just genital oriented. By knowing yourself from head to toe, you will bring a deeper dynamic into play when you finally partner for sex.

Just as our spiritual life leads us to know thyself — the sexual side of our being follows this same principle. Many can, have and do engage sexually with others without a full understanding of their own sexuality. If touching themselves was frowned upon during early childhood and later, it is apparent that it would be best to go back in time with one's self and begin pleasurable touching while in solitude.

For some, it may help to use a method where you pretend to be another person's hand pleasuring yourself. This fantasy can place you as the innocent learning and your hands as the curious explorer, thus teaching you exactly what turns you on the most and how. Doing this with all of the body and not just the genital area is preferred. We have nerve endings

everywhere! Just having your feet or hands stroked or massaged can send signals waking you up to greater potentials. Your skin is the largest living organ of your body and as it begins to awaken from slumber and is touched, a desire for the sexual act will awaken.

Remove all distractions during this time with yourself such as phones, televisions, etc. Music is fine and perhaps beneficial for many. The goal is to make this your "me time" wherein you are not going to be disturbed. However, another aspect of this time with yourself is to remove all preconceptions you have about touching and sensuality. Therefore, it would not behoove you to visually watch images you are attracted to in order to gain an aroused state. Initially, arousal is not a goal but if it occurs this is fine. Orgasm is not a goal either. Begin slowly with yourself and have several sessions like this.

In the first few sessions, you may want to focus solely on your upper torso and head. Massage your scalp and the back of your neck. Try lightly stroking your face or certain areas of your neck and shoulders. Everything is for your pleasure and this is a wonderful thing. Many empaths are so focused on concern of their partner's pleasure during the act that they will even end a sexual encounter early if they feel it may be taking them too long to reach a satisfactory climax. We will talk more of that later. The point here is to really relax into the fact that your spirit has been encased in this physical body and it is time to show it some love via touching.

While engaged in these touching sessions, do not have a final goal of any kind such as climax. If that happens, wonderful, but how about continuing the touching all over the body for a while longer? Movement and stretching of muscles and limbs may also feel good. There are no rules as each person discovers in depth what makes them feel good.

Taking this time, guilt-free, is very important for empaths who often need this type of tactile grounding. This can assist with feeding the sensual earthy side of one's self instead of stuck "in the head" so much in the higher chakras. This is part of a beautiful balancing between mind and body. Those who have been traumatized or victims of sexual abuse will also find this private time very beneficial in getting in touch again with one's own sexuality. It is important to make this time to treat yourself and regain your sensuality, even if carnal in one sense.

Without intense details, you can envision that learning to pleasure yourself from head to toe is training you to be a better lover — not for what your partner will want, but for communicating what you like to that person in an easier manner.

No matter who you are, the dizzying pace we live at now where multitasking can seem to be a prerequisite for existing, taking this private time for yourself holds multiple health benefits. For everyone, just the pleasure of touch can release endorphins in the brain making your mood feel happier and much brighter. If arousal occurs during touch exploration, oxygen levels are increased to the brain.

Many empaths find themselves embroiled in the wrong relationships too quickly and often with a sexual encounter. By becoming masterful at your own sensual pleasure, it can be much easier to wait until you know this person is right for you to couple with. You do not need their sexual energy to feel complete, as you have taught yourself to use fantasy and touching to gift that to yourself.

Another benefit is that things happen in life where you may find yourself without a partner to be sexual with. People die. They are in accidents or experience illnesses that leave them in a state of being unable to engage in an encounter. Staying with that person in a relationship should not be based

solely upon sex. In case of something tragic, being comfortable with pleasuring one's self could be very important in this situation as well.

If the empath is paired sexually with someone suffering from a severe personality disorder such as the malignant narcissist or sociopath, true enjoyment on a deep, satisfying level will be impaired. Here the empath may find that an old story line in their life is fulfilled somehow with this individual. Many dynamics can be at play here that could revolve around early experiences in life of receiving and giving love on any level. When an empath is with one of these individuals affected with a personality disorder, the balance of the sexual encounter will be off. It will definitely be one in which the affected person has no problem finding gratification. However, the empath will be left wanting in most situations. When they are not, it is because there is a mental tension which produces a different type of excitement for the encounter. It is feeding a victim mentality somewhere in the makeup of the empath. They could actually view this as very desirable sex unless and until they experience something that makes this seem like child's play with another more balanced individual.

A question I received from a reader was the sensation she experienced after emotional or sexual involvement with someone wherein she was left feeling sad. First, this is an excellent question in general. More importantly, I love the fact that she, as an empath, is checking in with her feelings after being with the other person. Often, an empath will be more concerned about how the other person is feeling after an interaction. The fact that she is honoring her emotions and noticing how she feels is a good sign. Why would you feel sad after a sexual encounter in particular? There are many things that could create this within the empath.

First, it could be as simple as something sad in the other individual's auric field or even sadness they hold within their own mind and body that the empath is absorbing during the

sexual act. If you are particularly psychic, you could be picking up on something very sad in their past or that person's future. This could be something tragic that happens to them or they imposed upon another. It could also be your higher self letting you know this is not a great match for you and will leave you feeling sad in the long run.

Another possibility is more related to physiology. There can be such a rush of endorphins and a feeling of connectedness with another individual during the sexual act. As the brain chemicals begin to normalize after the act, this could be felt as a "coming down" off the high produced during your time together. One way to test this is to encourage or ask your partner to spend a little time in the afterglow period with you wherein you are still hugging, touching, stroking each other's shoulders or back, making eye contact and perhaps even laughing together. If this seems to solve the feelings of sadness, you will know this is probably the cause.

Yet another reason someone may feel sad after intimacy could be more complex. This may involve deeply ingrained patterns from early sexual experiences or taboo thought patterns held from upbringing. If the empath has been sexually abused, this could also be a culprit of negative feelings after the sexual act. To determine if this is the case, it will take much self analyzing and reflection.

Remember that when we join with another physically, we are not only exchanging bits of our DNA with that individual, but also bits of our life force. There is a light cord connecting the two of you. The strength of that cord depends upon the emotional intensity coming from one or both of you. Those emotions can be positive and loving or rooted in fear and attachment.

Your body is your temple and it does not have to stay a sacred virginal spot, but one that is shared with thought and reverence. This leads to the best sexual experience for all.

16 - Perceptions & Beliefs

"The best years of your life are the ones in which you decide your problems are your own. You do not blame them on your mother, the ecology, or the president. You realize that you control your own destiny." ~ Albert Ellis

Where do our beliefs come from? There are several ways we form them. The first is through the causal reactions we encounter being mothered as an infant. Our perceptions about things lead to beliefs. Our beliefs often lead to judgments we hold about our self or others.

It is amazing how several different individuals can visually see an event occur and each will have a separate perception of it. This is because each person picked up only certain things that stood out to them the most. If they went back and watched the entire incident on video, even pausing it or slowing it down at some sections, their judgments about the incident would change because they now had a wider area and more time to perceive the incident.

If you stood on a busy city sidewalk and took a survey of the opinions of passerby's on something that is in the news quite a bit, a particular political figure or issue, you would get quite a few judgments coming from many of the participants. Repeat phrases and catch words might be included in their responses. This is because they are being told what to think in subtle and sometimes overt ways via numerous media sources.

In reality, each individual has based their judgments upon the perceptions they have gained from these other sources that want to influence their opinions.

Throughout our lives, the way we perceive other people and situations can completely color our own experience. We can see the world a certain way after time. It is healthy and good to challenge our perception of many things from time to time. This keeps us in a free thinker mode instead of a programmed one.

Allow me to paraphrase a social media posting I saw that made me very sad. The young woman posting stated that she wears a smile but behind it, she is living in pain. She described this as mental pain that has now become physical. Her mental condition is complex post traumatic stress disorder.

Her main complaints in the posting were that she is tired of the system and does not fit in. She claims most people around her are sleeping and not aware like she is to the very sick society we live in. She claims capitalism was created to destroy humanity and our planet. All of this triggers her C-PTSD. Her largest trigger is oppression. Her view is that we live in a world dominated by rape, racism, abusive marriages, class inequalities, and just all around world suffering.

Even though this makes her feel like she cannot breathe, she says she keeps smiling. She feels she is part of the resistance and she is here to spread love even though she claims her heart is sometimes full of hate and anger. In fact, she just wants to explode at times. She says the reason for her posting is that she just wants more of us to do the same as she is doing.

When I read her post, I saw a person in pain and it is very sad. She is using the guise of good will and for her friends to be "awake" to gain attention for how badly she really hurts. Without knowing it, I believe it is possible she has turned that part of her that has judged herself harshly into now judging the world.

I happen to know quite a bit about C-PTSD, although not an expert. I did suffer from it severely in the past. All of it coming from trauma wounds. I can still be triggered but have overcome much. Many of you hearing these words suffer from it now or have in the past.

First, we must acknowledge this person who posted will only post what they feel they want revealed publically. Second, she is coming from a position of little to no power. If this is how she is really operating day to day, why would anyone want to be this powerless? There is a lot of blaming going on. There is a need to make division lines, judgments against others and such. I would say she has a desire to spread love but will not be able to do so effectively with so much hate and anger she claims is in her most of the time.

I will say what I believe could be the case for this young woman. She has been indoctrinated to have a high weight on horrible things going on worldwide. It is easy to have this happen. I personally am triggered by human and child slavery and trafficking. Yet, I have to keep in perspective that, while it is large in scope, it is not going on everywhere all the time. I do not become depressed about it. I do something to actively help those affected with my free podcast to assist in healing the emotional aspects of sexual abuse. We have to take back our power in ways that we can find useful to ourselves and others. By taking lemons and turning them into lemonade, all may benefit if they desire to.

With the programming and indoctrination process that is going on educationally for many, people are using certain circumstances in the world to demonize particular groups of individuals. This is not loving and it does not help humankind evolve in any manner. With discernment, it really does not take long to break it all down common sense wise if one is willing

to look at it. Hate and division are being fostered and taught to people in the guise of love. Love does not behave that way. Justice and circumstances are not always fair and often the real facts about situations are not presented to the general public. Instead, we have a version of what the program masters what the populace to believe.

What can happen is people only see the world through the filter they have been provided. An analogy might be that you are only exposed to the news on television each day. That is the only thing really happening in your world. You never hear about good things going on or that there is a new organization to help blind people or something similar. You only hear the bad news. Now, you are sick yourself from being fed this. You are angry. You want change. The paradox of this is that we each must be the change — be the real change. We only heal our world when we heal ourselves. We grow through adversity and fixing our own inner self. We do not expect other people or the world to change for us. That is a violation of free will.

Do you know that we have always had oppression on this planet? Do you know that true empaths, starseeds, indigo and crystals are here to be helpers of these conditions? We have been born here for varied purposes and at a critical time in history. Yet, all times of this planet have held battles between the dark and light in this duality.

Let's look at what we know of history on Earth regarding oppression. This will show you how capitalism is not the culprit, but plain old control — often through bloodlines of individuals. From the Greek and Roman eras to the Middle Ages in Europe, control has been an issue. Rulers by blood connection enacted the laws and circumstances people would live under. It was present during the time of Jesus Christ, moving through each century and remaining through the industrial age. Now, in the age of technology, never has control and domination of the people been more apparent.

You see, the face or outer wrapping of this domination changes, but not the core essence of it. Capitalism, while not perfect, is the reason so many worldwide want to come to the United States of America. Unfortunately, our systems have become infected and corrupted with thought patterns that this way of life is the problem. In reality, it is a deeper, hidden controlling force behind all systems of government — one that they now wish to pull into one world domination under the guise of socialism, very quickly leading to communism. This is complete slavery of the people in my opinion and goes against everything I stand for spiritually.

Any time you are not able to live freely, you are a slave. I hold a vision of those under the spell of the false indoctrination that they discern how damaging it is and break free from it quickly. We must not be tricked into a very sad state of a world.

Consciousness

Our early experiences create a filter through which we see events, people and the world. Each of us has a colored experience. We are literally walking around experiencing the world one way when a change of filter could make it appear completely different. Nowhere is this more apparent than when we experience different states of consciousness.

Within all indigenous cultures of Earth, there have always been those that naturally were able to alter their conscious state at will. Many times they availed the help of dancing, drugs, movement or extreme stillness and silence. This still goes on today. Always, there was a point they were waiting for … a place between the waking state of that which you sense directly around you now and not quite the dream state where we seem to have a hard time being immersed in the physical.

The quest always is for this delicate state between the two worlds of wakefulness and deep sleep - a place that is created by a vibration called Theta waves. This is not some type of new age dogma, although they know about it. It is science. When measured, theta waves resonate at 4-8 Hz. The time you are most likely to experience this state is when highly focused mentally which we often find with people practicing prayer, meditation or some other type of spiritual practice. Deep trance meditation can certainly produce theta waves.

When a human brain is functioning at the theta level, the feeling could be described as almost asleep but almost awake. It is that state you may find yourself in as you come out of a dream toward wakefulness. One could feel "stuck in a dream" if they wake and are primarily in a theta wave mode. Children have the capacity to experience theta waves normally. Sometimes, children will slip into this theta consciousness easily while daydreaming. Did you ever lie in the grass as a child, perhaps twisting clover in your hands and watch the clouds? At a time like that, theta waves are very possible for a child.

Why is changing our conscious state beneficial at times? Just as someone may need a change of scenery such as a vacation or a change of people, our minds need to wander into new territory as well. What we are around switches our outlook, colors things differently as we absorb the different energies of our new environment. How do we change this on demand when we know we are living in a situation where we are stuck and feel we cannot? Silence and nature time are critical to hear the messages of your soul.

How Spirit Speaks To Some

Not everyone wants to or can be a medium or a voice for spirit. Many empaths are extremely intuitive and even telepathic with humans, but they never entertained the idea that sometimes, when the conditions are right, they could have also been picking up thoughts, images and signals from spirit. There are different types of mediumship. Mental mediumship is a natural gift where you are picking up on the thoughts of others whether they are in this dimension or elsewhere. It is a type of telepathy.

Channeling is a verbal medium with a shift from the left brain to the creative receptive right brain. A person who channels conveys information to others via their voice or in writing that is beyond their personal knowledge.

Artistic mediumship is when a person can see using their mind's eye instead of their regular vision. They may draw images or perhaps only see particular colors that clue them into something they did not know prior.

Many tools can be used for accessing the unknown and finding answers or clues. Divination has been used for thousands of years from divining rods to find water to runes, stones, and cards. Scrying with mirrors, reflecting water, or crystal balls is another method of allowing the tool to show you. For best results with any of these tools, that same process of shifting the brain from analytical to intuitive is best. Allow your awareness to bring forth thoughts, words, and images. Trusting the process is an important part of your psychic development. To know and stand firmly on the information you receive is a part as well.

Children often come into the world with gifts that are almost always abated by adults. Children are natural healers and empathizers. They can have an inner discernment about people such as good guy / bad guy unknowingly. Animals often display this ability also. You may have observed this with

dogs, cats or other animals. Essentially, adults teach us to not trust ourselves as children and follow our intuition. Look how long it takes to turn that around!

17 - Vibration

"Concerning matter, we have been all wrong. What we have called matter is energy, whose vibration has been so lowered as to be perceptible to the senses. There is no matter."

~ Albert Einstein

The subject of vibration is simple, yet multi-layered and complex in its detail. You are well acquainted with the concept because it involves energy. I repeat various attributes of it simply because we seem to often need quick review and a deepening of our understanding on a continual basis. The world we inhabit can seem so solid and real — yet it is all energy vibrating at various frequencies.

This can be thought of as different channels on a radio or television. You bring in a particular station by changing stations — dialing up or down. Chances are you have a particular station where you stay most of the time. You have options on your radio. You can bring in static, less clear frequencies such as AM or clearer FM or digital frequencies. You can watch cable on your television and switch to live streaming digital if desired. Social media has its own vibe or resonance. This can differ from user to user depending on what is appearing in your news feed; groups you belong to; people you have friended or followed. All engagement with elements like this has effects upon us. You can adjust the way these platforms and devices are affecting you by choosing what you will allow on them. It just depends on the devices (tools) you

have at your disposal. So it is with your body/mind/spirit complex.

You also have within your mind/body/spirit complex the ability to enjoy different levels of vibration simultaneously. According to the Hermetic teachings, the mental plane contains seven corresponding categories of vibration or existence and seven subcategories for each of those seven resulting in seven squared or forty-nine vibratory levels in the mental plane alone. There are also two additional planes in addition to the mental plane, that being the physical and spiritual. These planes of existence also have seven categories and seven subcategories.

Important Reminder - thought is always vibrating faster than light. Light is always vibrating faster than sound.

For practical purposes and keeping your feet on the ground, you must be conscious of where you are vibrating or resonating more of the time. You do this by checking in with your senses, particularly your emotions, but all senses are involved. Part of more consciously creating your reality is to choose carefully and deliberately what you will tune into. What frequencies are you tuned into? What do you allow yourself to be exposed to?

Many of the divisive talk radio programs and panel debates on television are really just negative reinforces. We hear arguments between different viewpoints on television that never produce real solutions. Exposing your mind to these activities too often does not enhance your ability to consciously manifest your positive goals. Some may choose to disconnect from these types of media for a period of time as an experiment to see how their conscious manifestation is affected. Remember, you are continually manifesting your reality with your thoughts and emotions. These types of programs on television and radio are programming individuals to often feel fear, anxiety, powerlessness to change our situations and world.

We have heard of the concept of "garbage in, garbage out" in speaking of computers and our brains. Be mindful of what frequencies are around you and every area of your life where you have a choice about this. It is critical to make the higher selection on the vibratory dial for yourself. To turn off these distractions will also intensify your ability to use intention — an integral part of consciously manifesting. Even the most adept must disconnect at times from the negative noise that is constantly pumped out. In fact, the most adept humans would not expose themselves very much at all to such things as the match-up — the resonance — is just not there for them.

You do not have to choose to completely stick your head in the sand or pretend that events do not exist. You can choose to quickly catch the headlines without getting into all the nuances and arguments of why a situation is happening, who is responsible; who is going to do something about it; or not.

You may also choose to send love to all those involved in tragedy. You may choose to donate goods or money. You may choose to sign a petition or actively campaign for a change. You may choose to meditate and hold a vision for the entire world of peace and abundance. All of those are real solutions moving forward to a higher vibration.

If you have developed an addiction to social media and the chaotic news programs, could you believe your reality is based upon everything that is being presented? You must find ways to wean yourself gently or abruptly so you may consciously manifest a better existence for yourself and others. As long as you stay hooked into this, part of your vibration is stuck there. Simply changing to books, audio or programming that is positive or even comedic will alleviate much of this. Watch yourself very carefully when a major event happens .... and they seem to occur weekly at times. From missing planes, weather disasters, riots, murders, accidents, wars, threats real or perceived, financial calamities and more, you are literally bombarded with lower vibrational thoughts which fuel lower vibrational emotions.

If you got in your vehicle, or a bus or train and went somewhere beautiful in nature for the day or a number of days where you were disconnected from it all, you would be stronger, more mentally focused and an overall happy individual.

For those of you that are surrounded by this type of media all the time as a journalist or something similar, you have chosen this and have the choice to stay in it or leave and do something different with your skills and knowledge. If you stay, perhaps you can be part of the solution. If your work structure is too restrictive for any flexibility, perhaps you can begin to explore and consciously manifest a new career and life for yourself.

What is the purpose of raising your vibration? This specifically correlates with the law of attraction. As your frequency ascends, so do the experiences you find yourself in. Suddenly, the synchronicities begin to occur. Opportunities present that are furthering you toward your conscious creation goals. Ideas and solutions emerge that did not exist before. Follow up on these, no matter how strange they may seem at the time.

As you raise your vibration, you will also have more command over emotions or moods. You will notice what items or people trigger you now and those that no longer bother you at all. You will learn to transcend these items or people … or to remove them as unnecessary interference. Being triggered can be thought of as a good thing because it shows you where you still need to do some healing and clearing of thoughts and feelings. Use this to your advantage. Ask *why does this impact me so much? What can I do about this moving forward?*

You have more control than you may realize in changing the frequencies or vibrations you are currently resonating with. However, you cannot be up all the time. All of us fall short and experience lower vibes and energy. It can be affected by events happening around us, people who hurt or betray us, systems that fail us. There are times when we do not know what to blame our mood upon. It is like we awoke in a fog. Our brain feels fuzzy and unfocused. This haziness can be like residue that needs to be washed away to find one's self again. Sometimes, water can provide that relief for us with its amazing properties to heal. A hot shower can bring us around to where we feel refreshed, renewed and more like crafting our day.

Remember in *Book I of The Magical Empath*, I mentioned many things we can do to change up our vibration — music, color, movement, affirmations, singing, chanting, moving, etcetera.

Resonate

Each of us has a different energy signature. Just as birds differ in their approach and how they experience life, humans vary like this as well. As a species, some of our energy patterns will be common. But our psychological and physical ways of giving out and receiving energy will imbue us with our own unique fingerprint.

We know there are ways to streamline certain things. Obviously some acts, words or thoughts are collectively agreed by the majority to be negative or positive. But, have you ever found out that you hurt someone's feelings by something you said; did; did not do? You were truly surprised by this and may think the other person was being too sensitive or blowing things out of proportion. To make that determination is a subjective exercise. It is only an opinion based upon what you

determine is reasonable and not within the other person's experience.

I remember being told often as a child that I was "taking things too personal"; "had a chip on my shoulder"; "needed to learn to take a joke"; and needed to "stop feeling sorry for myself". Perhaps the adults around me that said this were right at times. Overall, there was a lack of empathy on their part. I was a very sensitive child that really did not understand why the people around me would do or say things I felt were hurtful — and then blame me for being hurt. This is called invalidation and it is a subtle form of abuse that many professionals feel is a very treacherous one.

Inside each of us, we carry these patterns of early conditioning. Now, as an older woman, I dearly love that little sensitive girl that still lives within my heart. I don't feel sorry for myself because I am no longer a child who is powerless to make change happen. Now, I feel strong. It took me years to heal from all the abuse from different sources. I did not just rise above situations. I worked to transmute them as much as possible.

Look at what could be affecting your vibration — something that is perhaps stuck there in a pattern from your past. Often, you can find the roots of it by listening to the clues your self-talk gives you. Take just one day and count as many times as you can what that part of your mind is saying to you. Write it down in brief terms. How does it make you feel? Remember that your thoughts are connected to the seventh chakra area. Another thing to notice is how much you are critical or judging others. Damn, this can be so revealing that you will want to avoid it at all costs. But, try it!

18 – Flow & Resistance

"Resistance is the first step to change." ~ Louise Hay

"Energy flows where intention goes." ~ Tony Robbins

There are many different examples of resistance in life and it will assist you to recognize them all. Resistance in its varied forms is not all bad or good. In fact, it is through periods of restriction where we sometimes have the most opportunity to grow in character. While this book focuses on manifestation of goodness and abundance, it is only through the dualities of plenty and scarce; love and fear; beauty and ugliness that we learn to differentiate and grow. This could be why we have many religions created in the past that encourage or require abstinence of some sort. From the sparse life of a monk, nun or priest, to the opulence of a billionaire, our world shows us the entire gamut of things …. monetarily, physically, mentally and spiritually.

Restriction is not always voluntary like when someone joins a convent, priesthood or even the military. It can be imposed by circumstances we unknowingly created or helped to create. Whether your restriction is monetary, physical or mental, look for the good in it and what you can gain from the experience. The faster you accomplish that, the sooner you may move onto less restriction, if that is what you desire.

Part of progressing as an actualized person is being aware exactly where your resistance exists and then figuring out why. Without doing this, you will operate in various stages of victim roles that are often your own self made obstacles, delay points, and for some a self imposed prison. It takes setting aside the ego personality that you want to believe you are — and convince others as well — to find these pockets of resistance and turn them into a flowing energy that eventually enhances you.

By identifying them in an honest way, you are able to see what could be reduced or eliminated so that life is flowing without feeling stuck or unable to navigate all the hurdles. Identification is not enough. You must also analyze what is holding these barriers in place, keeping you from your best experience. Some resistance is beneficial and necessary to keep us from going off the rails.

When a surge of electricity flows freely and does not meet with resistance (an electrical resistor), it is said to be a superconductor. If a resistor is present, it could have a mild effect on the flow of the electrical current if it is classified as a conductor. Common conductors can be metals such as silver, gold, copper or aluminum. These conductors are mild resistors indicating they are easier for the electrons to pass through. If the resistor is more of the insulating variety, its molecular structure will be more difficult for the electrons to flow through and there is more energy loss experienced in the electrical flow. There is less energy passing through the thicker or greater the resistance (Fluke, 2021).

With increased resistance, there is only one way that you can overcome this challenge: to pass more electrical flow through. You would need to increase the original voltage at the beginning (Iowa State Univ., n.d.).

Drawing that same parallel with the human mind/body/spirit complex, you would need to increase the

amount of life force energy at the point of origin where it enters you in order to have a chance of flowing through resistance and still maintaining an equal or higher amount of energy (life source) once it is passed. If you have energy flowing through you that is not impeded and moving like an irresistible force, this could eventually be weakening to your mind/body/spirit complex. And this brings up the ways that resistance can actually serve to somewhat slow down these rapid firings of life force energy.

Resistance is not all bad and some is necessary. To have the right amount of resistance helps to buffer the experience to what is palatable or tolerable based on where you are currently in your growth. The right amount of resistance can keep your system from overload and shock. Yet, when resistance is too high, we stay on a lower level of personal achievement and growth due to what could be termed as an invisible blockage or tough passageway to travel through (Physics Stack Exchange, 2013).

All electrical systems need to be grounded to keep from shorting out. Likewise, your human system must have grounding also. As empaths, we can spend much time stuck in the upper chakras, ignoring the needs of the lower ones. Feeling secure and stable is the role of the first chakra and it would be beneficial to check in occasionally to see if you are experiencing any blockages there or over activity. Balancing the chakras on a regular basis will keep your energy flowing well without that type of resistance.

Checking in with one's self, the first step is recognizing where you feel this invisible tug of war. Look first at what zaps your energy or blocks your potential. This could be on a physical, spiritual or mental level. Ultimately, the entire mind/body/spirit complex is afflicted with the resistance you have identified. There are clues to finding what is depleting your energy and holding you back. For instance, how much we care about something is often equal to the resistance you have

the capacity to create about that subject matter. Is the resistance mild and healthy for you in its limitations or is it restricting and holding you back?

Another clue to finding what you are resisting is to acknowledge what you hold the most emotion around. This is where you will find the little damns in the energy river that have been created without you knowingly participating. What plugs up the experience of going with the flow? Generally speaking, it is thoughts. These thoughts are the culmination of fears and self doubt. It can also be programmed patterns of misguided principles present in the world around us. Many of these ideas have been perpetuated by our family of origin. It is important to note that your thoughts can cement themselves into attitudes and behaviors that totally represent the resistance.

I remember my father, a Scorpio, insisting that I needed a plan. Logical thought was at the basis of everything and each decision. I needed to "get my head on straight". Most of all, I needed that plan for my life. Now, I have nothing against life planning, but I think plans are better when they are fairly general and have room for flexibility.

What Creator Source can bring me is always going to be much more fulfilling and interesting than what I can dream up on my own. Plus, when I start getting really detailed with the plan and trying to control a lot of it, this is where all that resistance begins to build. And, I'm doing it all with my own thoughts. So, yes, my dad is right. Everyone needs some kind of plan, but it should be one born of our internal desires with room for our guiding force to show us what the steps are that lead to the eventual outcome we have been visualizing.

My father also emphasized that all of this would be hard — a struggle to just stay afloat in this world. There would be sacrifices of making myself study things I may not be ready for or even interested in. He insisted that is where the jobs are. My father entered the work force at a time when people did not

make career changes. In our current world climate, you need to be ready to change careers at least each decade, if not sooner, because things are changing constantly in our world. If vocations are not being replaced by robots and AI, they are outsourced or eliminated.

Father wanted me to be "practical". There is nothing more rewarding, productive or practical than joining forces with God/Goddess/All That Is to allow guidance toward my desires. If I can stay focused (there's that word again) on that beautiful connection, things flow and fall into place. If I allow myself to begin thinking negative thoughts like:

- What if this does not happen?
- I might be keeping someone else from their good or purpose.
- I have to be realistic.
- I must be more practical.
- I must accept the way it is in this world.

All of the above fears and thoughts block flow. They create resistance. Those types of thoughts keep you from aligning with your higher purpose. There is nothing more satiable and satisfying than being relaxed and in the flow. Feeling as if you are floating at sea and your final destination is a beautiful place where your desires culminate as you have been directing in a relaxed fashion. Being in the flow is not always present for us. By golly, when it happens for you, take that wave, ride it and go. It is not the time to hem and haw over it. Just do it and go with your flow. When we are in our flow, we feel our most authentic and jubilant. This is the time when you know yourself at a deep level and feel trusting and confident that you are moving in the right direction.

If I just tell God Source, please guide me to do what is going to fulfill my purpose, make me prosperous and happy — now that is a plan. Who could want for more than that, really? All the main ideas are going on in that plan: fulfill purpose; happy and prosperous. There is plenty of room for this to be an adventure inspired by Creator Source, rather than a drudgery thought up from the human source.

So how does this work in the 3D environment you are in? Suppose you hate your job but you need it to pay your bills. Here is what I would do, step by step:

First, realize that in order to make any change toward something you will be happier, prosperous and fulfill your purpose, there must be a transition period of time. Some transitions can happen instantly — like you won the lottery and are now free to pursue whatever your heart desires. Most transitions take some time. This requires that you actively hold faith that what you desire will happen in the perfect timing for you.

1) Ask God Source to show you a way to transition to something that you love doing that makes you feel full inside — as in fulfilling your purpose. Then wait, keep your intuition open and wait for little urges, nudges, synchronicities and signs.

2) Sit down with some quiet time for yourself and figure out what you want. Do this no matter how unrealistic it seems. It is important to write it down and keep it somewhere special — but a place where you will read it often and perhaps even amend it from time to time.

3) Once you know what you want, begin diving deep to ask why do I want that? What does it bring me? How would it make me feel if I had it?

4) When ideas or opportunities come to you and it feels good - act on them.

Let me give you an unusual example so that you can see how you often shut yourself down. Let's say the thought occurs to you that you want to become a tap dancer. You have always loved watching old movies with people tap dancing and you love the rhythm and sound that can occur just from the feet. Immediately, you could begin having thoughts like:

No one is going to pay me to tap dance.

No one cares about tap dancing.

This is just a crazy idea.

But, what if you didn't do that and you instead immediately bought a pair of tap shoes and began practicing at home after work? What if you then enrolled in a dance school to learn tap dancing? What if you became better and better through practice and then began making videos at home or at your dance studio of you performing tap dancing in a unique way? What if you uploaded those videos and became an Internet sensation when it comes to tap dancing? What if you made people smile and shake their heads in amazement with your tap dancing? What if your name became a household word because of your tap dancing? What if you were then invited to use your name to host a television show where contestants come on and they tap dance with you as a judge? What if you then used your name to license tap dancing schools across your country or the world? What if you were offered licensing fees for a line of dance apparel? By now, you have quit your job and have lots of wealth and opportunities derived from your original crazy idea of tap dancing. What if you hired an inventor/designer to produce tap shoes that not

only lit up with multi-colors, but also produced even wilder sounds than the original tap shoe? Do you see how this works?

All of a sudden, people are engaging in an activity that you could have shut down with a single resistant thought, but instead decided to pursue. You did not know where it would lead. You just went with the impulsive thought. Your family and friends thought you were crazy when you told them you were going to be a tap dancer. Some told you to get your head out of the clouds … come back down to earth. Some just flat out said you cannot make money tap dancing — it's an old dance style that people no longer want.

You must really get this in your mind now because this is what we do to ourselves on a constant basis. We are being guided toward something that is good for us and will bring us toward our purpose, prosperity and joy. However, we shut it down with our negative thoughts or those around us whom we allow to create self doubt. All of this represents resistances — blockages to the good awaiting one's self.

If you say, yeah, you're right. No one cares about tap dancing. Wonder if I can sell these shoes to someone? This is how we kill dreams and desires. If you desire prosperity, joy and inner fulfillment, you must chase these impulsive, unplanned, non thought out crazy desires that arise out of nowhere because they are coming from a genius much greater than yours. They are often the beginning of a path that leads to somewhere much greater than the detailed strategy plan you think you need to develop. This is why you hear wise people say, "Follow your bliss." It is there that you will find what you are looking for.

On the way to trying to walk a magical life path, I realized I needed to unlearn many things. I came into my adult life with the preconception that I would need to get a certain amount of required education and work jobs I did not like to survive. Life a fish out of water, I flip flopped around with

whether I could even live like this. We have all done work we did not like and many are still doing it "to survive". But, what if I told you there really is another way?

I sold real estate for thirteen years and had my own brokerage with agents for five of those years. During that time, I enjoyed what I did most of the time and the financial rewards were great. However, in my core, I knew it was not what I really wanted to do. In my mind, I envisioned that later I would be a writer ... and a gardener. I would write books about subjects I loved and when I lost any of my inspiration, I would head to the garden to gather more ideas by allowing my hands to contact the earth's soil and drink in the whispers from flowers. My husband always believed in my ability to write. He did not know how it all works, what is required and I did not know how it would happen. I just knew that this is what I envisioned for myself.

Years ago, I printed out a few positive statements and placed them on my wall. One in particular spoke of being one's self and how that was the key to abundance. I would read it at times and think how can that be? I wanted to believe it was true, but could not figure out all the logical components of how this happens. It really wasn't my time. Unknowingly, I would go through a total transformation over the next decade and looking back now, it was required for me to be who I truly am now and to step into that role.

Another quote on the wall was "do what you love and the money will follow." This statement left me with two options: quit what I was doing and let my bills pile up or find a way to get paid for doing something I loved. It took some time, hardships and occasional fails, but I now do what I love. What I learned through all of this is that our focus and thoughts are constantly bringing our reality about in a huge way that we cannot fathom. We hear this, but do we see how deep it is? Focus, particularly is important because what consumes us or predominates our thoughts is what we often see happening

around us. Many of us have heard the saying, "what you resist, persists". This is true because we keep running up against the same road blocks. There is a continual leakage of energy as well at these points of resistance.

Further, the things we resist keep coming toward us on the wheel of life until we have mastered those items. In some strange circle dance, we cannot seem to rid ourselves of that situation or encounter until we have finally learned its lessons and made the necessary changes so that it is never attracted to us again.

When we can put our desires at the forefront and only focus on that with enthusiasm, expectancy and intent, we have an excellent chance of it manifesting for us. Instead of focused on what is not working, what is logical, what is quick, we must focus intently on what we want to come to us and then don't try to control that with a detailed plan. Have a loose plan and allow the universe to bring it to you in its own way which will always be ten times better than the detailed plan you could have come up with.

Here is another way of looking at it. In the business of writing fiction, some people outline and fill out in great detail the background of each character, scenes within the story; etcetera. These writers are called planners. Other writers are called "pansters", meaning they just sit down with only an idea and begin writing by the seat of their pants. In the middle of the two are those referred to as "plansters" who use a loose outline that has a lot of room for movement and change within the story. They begin with a basic idea that has a level of comfortable structure, but allow the details to flow to them as they work on the project.

This third approach is the one you want to take when it comes to fulfilling your dreams. Allow universal energy to do the work for you. Don't feel like you have to have every little

detailed planned out. Be flexible, with a loose structure of your desires and follow your intuition.

All of this comes down to self love again, because you see yourself as not worthy enough to be bestowed by fantastic ideas that will carry you financially and will give you all you desire, love and want. Instead, you might feel you must figure out a plan. You must sacrifice and work hard. If you feel like this, you have just identified a major point of resistance. Yet, hard work and some sacrificial choices are sometimes required to follow your best life. The difference is that when you are doing something you love, it won't feel so draining. Time flies by and before you know it, you have accomplished much because you actually enjoy the tasks in front of you.

The emotional connection is the key that unlocks the manifesting door for people. It is common for many to spend time with negative ideas floating through their brains. They create feelings of being worried, anxious, feeling left out, despair, pity and more. Then, they wonder why they cannot get those desires written in their journal or on their vision board to happen. They are confusing the universe. On the one hand, they are telling it to deliver them upon a path that leads to these wonderful feelings they will experience from owning the house in the mountains or at the beach; or having the career or partner they always wanted. They put that in their journal or their vision board. And then, they just sort of think of it periodically. In the meantime, they spend most of their time worried that they are not ever going to see their dreams come true. This is where their emotions lie most of the time — in a state of resistance. This is where they are resonating. This is where they will manifest from.

Visually move yourself into the higher emotions of already having exactly what you desire or something better. Do this now — before you have it. Generate feelings of gratitude and abundance, knowing with a strong faith that everything you desire or something even better is coming toward you.

Deeper methods to find how you are staying in a cycle of lack or that you are in a rut and cannot bust out is by looking at your habits, routines and how much you engage in procrastination. Again, these all reveal resistance. What are you not being responsible (responsive) about? What are you not handling in your life? By analyzing how you are allowing habitual ways of living to usurp your ability to manifest the good stuff in your life, you can see where you are unknowingly applying resistance.

Doubt

There are many times in life when it can be difficult to determine the right way to go. You come to a particular fork in the road and you know a decision has to be made, but you worry about making the wrong choice. This often can turn into procrastination as you begin to just dwell in this worried state. Indecision can also be a way of resisting our good. Determine what you need to do to move past that point. What does your intuition tell you about the situation? What feels like the most fulfilling path or decision you could make in the situation? What do you fear when it comes to one choice over the alternative one? These are the questions that will help you get past this and move forward.

Faith

You may have begun with feelings of hope that something will be better or come to fruition. When you have some success working these universal laws and principles, you will begin to see your hope turn into faith. Keep going and open the communication line between you and your Creator God for an unshakable faith that truly has the power to move things in ways you could never have imagined before. You have a dream about something and you do not know how it will

come together. You hold onto this dream with a strong faith that one way or another — that or something even greater you will love will happen. Faith is like an emotional fuel for your beliefs. Learn to recognize when you have been gifted with it through different experiences. Then, cultivate it. Once you hold a strong faith, it will be easy to ignore naysayers.

Gratitude

If there is one feeling you can generate, an emotion that will jump start good things coming toward you, it is gratitude. Each time we feel genuinely grateful, we attracting healing and a little more happiness into ourselves. There are times when it is so difficult to feel grateful because our inner self is out of balance at the time. Yet, even science is proving that it is well worth the small amount of time and effort it takes to generate emotions of gratitude.

Physiologically, filling your inner self with gratitude relaxes your muscles and you smile more easily. I am sure you have heard that it takes more facial muscles to frown and it is true. When you feel thankful, you also feel more connected to your God Source and loved. Your focus or charge switches to positive on your meter. Things seem brighter around you in terms of outlook. You are more likely to manifest abundance in your life at this time because you are setting the resonance — the atmosphere or vibration for attraction of it.

Even in the darkest of situations, there is something to be grateful for. It can and probably will be difficult to see it — especially while in the midst of it. Yet, it is there in even the most tragic of events.

Right at this moment, your human body is breathing and even if you are ill, there are thousands of truly miraculous processes occurring physically that you remain unaware of. These processes go on automatically to support you and work

toward your healing and homeostasis continually. I think of them within my own body from time to time and give thanks, noting that everything is working so well.

Have you ever noticed that if we have one thing in our body not working correctly that we obsess about it? We ignore everything else, thousands upon thousands of things that are working. Perhaps if we simply acknowledge what is out of balance, or not right, and make a plan to try and fix it and/or seek help from professionals who can help us heal. Focus more on what is working with our body systems to sustain us each second, whether we are awake or asleep. Feeling true gratitude for what is "right" in us or another is one way we can speed healing and definitely change focus.

Any person that has lost limbs, vision, hearing or some other major function can start to focus on what faculties they do have, being grateful for those and remaining open to receiving help from others. When such physical challenge is present, the only way forward is a process of grieving, sometimes anger, acceptance and finally, making the most of what is still working for that individual in order to move forward in life.

These individuals with physical and mental challenges are often admired for not allowing their circumstances to defeat them or take their spirits down a dark, lonely path that is ultimately destructive.

Perhaps you have been told that you have a terminal condition and given only a certain time frame you may live. How are you going to respond? Some told this have defied the doctors and even experienced spontaneous healings. Some have found a lifestyle or path that helped them to heal.

I am definitely not suggesting that anyone should ignore body symptoms or systems that are in distress, dis-ease or not working correctly. This is the body's way of saying it needs healing. What I am saying is that it is important not to

become hyperfocused on that particular issue, ignoring everything that is going right — the thousands of processes in your human system (known and unknown) that continue to work like clockwork.

We should all be striving to seek healing and remedies whenever possible on three levels: physical - mental (thoughts and emotions) and spiritual.

You can apply this process to any area of your life, not just your body. Identify problems, resistance in your career, education, organizations you are part of; relationships; finances; partnerships and more. Subsequently, notice and think about what is working — what is going right. There is hidden value in everything. Look for it — feel grateful for it often. By doing so, you change your vibration to a higher resonance.

Change

Giving up resistance requires change — pure change in habits of thinking or living. Once you know a point of resistance, you can analyze what needs to change about you in order to lessen its effect so that your life force may flow. Here is an example:

I recently reorganized all my books. One that I had for a number of years and have not read for awhile was about detoxing the body. I pulled it out and sat it upon my desk to skim through later and decide what detox plan I wanted to commit to in the near future. For days, the book just sat there unread. I realized there was a part of me that wanted to do this detox, but another that did not. I was experiencing resistance. I have fasted and detoxed before and knew the restriction and discipline involved. During a detox, it is common to not feel very great as toxins are being released. Yet, I had to laugh at myself that I was reluctant to read the book because that may

seem like a real commitment. Another part of me knows this change would be so beneficial.

- What are some of the reasons we resist change?
- Fear of living differently - even for a limited amount of time
- Fear of failing - falling off the regimen required
- Letting go of habits that have been toxic BFF's
- Afraid we will not have the willpower and worrying what it says about us if we do not
- Desire to avoid strife, unpleasant feelings/emotions
- Desire to avoid any struggle or uncomfortable situations

When you look over this collection of reasons we avoid change, you see that fear is involved. Fear of failing, struggles, being different, coming up against difficult feelings or not having enough willpower or discipline to follow through. It also involves leaving that comfortable place we have carved out where things no longer serving us suddenly seem like doing away with our BFF. But, we do not want those best friends .... forever. The fact that particular blockages or points of resistance you have are your best friends you cannot give up is an illusion. The only thing that gives the illusion any power is continuing to hang onto the idea.

Often, human mind trickery is involved as we adopt half truths about our obstacles that allow us to believe the lie. The real truth of the situation is unpleasant, even painful, to embrace. If we just close our eyes and do not look at what price resistance is charging us, we can be more at ease and not have to make a bunch of changes. That price for peace will take a heavy toll. It shows up in relationships with others and our internal feelings about us. It is the call of the song that was not

written or performed. It is the longing you cannot put your finger on that keeps you feeling terribly unfulfilled in life.

To remove resistive blocks, one could find one's self analyzing how this piece of lead got in the way to begin with. This can dredge up many issues from the past that probably need healing. Try not to sit with this alone, especially if we are speaking of past trauma. Reach out to others who can be an ear, a shoulder, a therapist or even a healer to transmute that which pains you. This healing work is critical, ultimately advancing you in removing resistance.

When we learned to walk, we fell down at times. We learned to catch ourselves with our hands; straighten back up and continue proudly practicing our new milestone skill. Metamorphosis is not easy for the caterpillar either. We enter the cocoon and during this dark time connect with our shadow sides of ourselves. It takes courage to go through this process and strip away all that we were to become our best self. Faith is required as we sit blind and still waiting for the big changes to happen when it seems that nothing is going to occur. Yet, we work on ourselves, squarely facing truths we wished we could avoid. Finally, we make the last changes necessary to emerge now with beautiful colors and wings that fly. For there is expansive freedom in living true to ourselves and making the hard choices to transform.

Suggested affirmation for change

I easily recognize habits I have fallen into and find new ways of operating and living that release me from the energy that has been stuck. Each time I replace negative patterns with more positive ones, I manifest my reality in a limitless way.

Notes – Thoughts – Ideas – Affirmations – Dreams

19 - Setbacks

"This too shall pass away." ~ King Solomon

We have all heard the idiom, *Against the Wind*. If life only subjected us to gentle breezes, we would really end up experiencing a rather mediocre life. Wind carves the mountains as does water. It spreads nurturing seeds to new territories of existence.

When the wind blows hard, we know we cannot resist it. We have two options: find shelter and wait for it to stop or "this too shall pass". We can also allow it to blow us along our path the course or direction it is taking. Obviously, we want to envision a life that is not wind-free, but filled with periodic breezes and not tornadic winds. Trees, flowers and all plant life are stronger because of the wind. Yet, when the wind is too violent, it can break those plants in half.

Empaths have always grown strong from the storms they have weathered. Adversity came along, but your trunk still stands like an ancient tree that has weathered much.

The corona virus pandemic has hit and created setbacks and disaster worldwide at the time of this writing. The entire world has been challenged in a way it was not before. Spring is upon us in the northern hemisphere and the birds singing outside have no knowledge of why the humans are a little less busy and abundant in numbers. Their survival and contentment relies upon tried and true rituals of nature which they were

taught by their mothers or know instinctively. There will be no help from the higher up birds if they fail to forge successfully on their own or happen upon a bitter poison. Nature is balanced, but it may not appear fair.

I think of this and look at the humans. So much blame they try to place on others. You must fix this or that for me now. That is what is fair and right. Why were you not totally prepared for this? Isn't this just abdication of responsibility?

What brings out the worst behavior in some kicks others into helpful emotional overdrive. They are the ones fixing situations, creating things that are needed, opening up avenues of help and wealth to others. Meanwhile, the others whine about even having to stay at home a couple of weeks. The fact about life is that disaster days can and will strike. Some days feel like an emotional catastrophe.

Has someone ever made you so angry you just felt a rage you never knew before? Perhaps the situation brought you to a point of either wanting to hurt something, someone or yourself. You may have found yourself slamming doors, speaking louder, even if no one is there to hear. If you have ever been at the edge like that, try to stop quickly! Grab a pen and begin writing. Who or what made you feel this way? What did they say or do — or not do? When did you notice these problems for the first time? How does all this make you feel?

Write it out dear soul. You can have confidence in knowing that others have felt just like you. When you have finished writing everything you can think of, feel, or even draw on the paper, please go to the next page. Write until your pen runs out of ink — then get another pen.

Finally, ask yourself what you are going to do in order to move forward and live a better life. You may want to wait until the next day, but begin to form on paper the following:

- What do you want — really want in life? Describe it.
- What kind of relationship is best for you?
- What would you like your friends to be like?
- What kind of friend could you be to others?
- Is there anything you want to change appearance wise?
- What kind of values do you cherish, if any?
- Is there something you really want?
- What types of places do you go?
- Where do you want to live?
- How much consistent income do you want and with what frequency?
- If you were to die soon, what do you want others to remember about you?

This may seem silly, but it redirects you now that your alignment has been shaken. It is time for you to feel better and working toward that which will bring you more joy. It does not have to be physical items, but that is okay if you want those things – perfectly fine.

We all have setbacks, delays, disappointments and outright horrible calamities. We must get back in the saddle though and ride carving out our journey to what really can be a magical life.

Notes – Thoughts – Ideas – Affirmations – Dreams

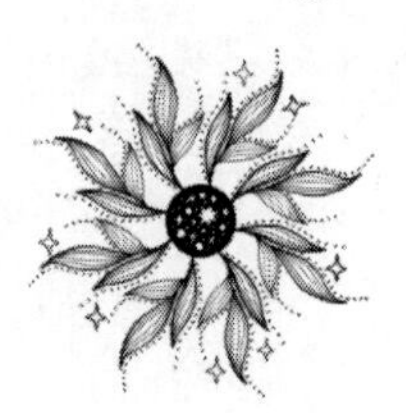

20 – Magical Personality

"Art is standing with one hand extended into the universe and one hand extended into the world, and letting ourselves be a conduit for passing energy." ~ Albert Einstein

The high vibrational state of being in your magical personality cannot be attained at all times. When you are in your magical personality, you are essentially drawing down your higher self. Since this spiritual part of you resides at a different density most of the time, using your magical personality is experienced for brief periods. Often, it can be increased in its intensity and duration by attracting it during favorable days or cycles of planetary positions. Some use ritual and objects to increase the effectiveness of slipping into this higher, magical state for a period of time. Yet, an adept can access this magical personality at any time of their choosing. The desire to do same is coupled with a strong intention and focused willpower.

Your intention and personal will can be quite ardent and developed to not need other accouterments to facilitate being in this state. Some are more naturally inclined at this and in that sense it could be called a gift. However, even those holding that ability naturally should not "rest on their laurels" or indulge their ego that they have no work to do. Natural talents and gifts unused and out of practice lose their luster. Often, they require a reactivation in order to be more pin point

with intentional co-creating and attracting desires. This would also involve regular use or practice.

Whether you were born with a natural propensity to have this magical quality of being able to create easily — positively or negatively — or you have had to work to develop your abilities, know this is a spiritual power you wield. Your spiritual power can be used in a positive manner which would reflect service to others or it can be used in a negative way that exhibits service to self mentality. The part of you that comprises this magical personality is leaning toward a positive or negative position in polarity. You may instantly know which way you lean. Or, you may have questions at times. How can you know for sure?

A negative polarity would show itself through various thought patterns and possibly actions and behaviors. One would need to examine if their thoughts or actions are oriented toward controlling others. Even if that same person puts up a false mask to act as if they do not want to control, but they really do and are manipulating circumstances covertly, this could be conceived by some as more egregious. It fits behavior that is self-serving. Many of us engage in this without even knowing it or why at times. Here is just one example:

Let's compare two individual situations. Person A is always giving of their time and talents to a disadvantaged youth organization. They boldly proclaim this philanthropic activity to others verbally, on their social profile page and even their resume. While they do enjoy working with the youth and helping out, the main intent is to look good for others in order to fulfill something they lack inside.

Person B also serves at the same youth organization but never mentions it to many people except perhaps close family and friends. This might even be more in the context of two scenarios. Perhaps a friend asks them to join for an activity on Saturday, but they are committed to the youth group that day.

They may mention this at the time. Another possible situation could be where they share the personal value they feel they have received by working with these youth, perhaps to offer it as a possible situation for another person to engage in.

Person A and Person B are both engaged in activities at the same organization that appear and can be service to others. With different motivations and intentions, each shows where they resonate on the scale. It should be noted that all true assistance, giving and help to the organization is valuable. Yet, to personally measure the polarity of an individual, they would need to look at their motivation or payoff. Person A needs an ego boost. Person B needs to feel good only inside of his or her self about their volunteer activities to feel as if they are fulfilling a purpose and contributing to the whole. They do not seek accolades but rather a desire to be helpful and of service.

Know yourself and what motives lie within your conscious awareness — explore this to determine where you are resonating. Some of the most giving people can use a type of martyrdom to influence others. The key is they are using it to affect the feelings, opinions or actions of others. Likewise, someone may seem selfish at times because they are taking care of their own needs first and putting up a boundary for another. This can be seen as service to self but it may be service to others. If we do not enact limitations or boundaries with others in our life, we run the risk of depleting ourselves and no longer being in a position to be of service or to give. We all must refill the well of our mind/body/spirit complex.

One key for the magical personality is to develop a longer attention span to be able to focus intently on your desires. There are different attention spans available to us. Our cognitive or intellectual span is one. Our spiritual attention span is another. You must work on both to walk a magical path in life. There is no need for perfection — just an awareness and dedicated practice of same. How do we increase our capacity to focus and hold our attention in time and space? For

advancement in the spiritual attention space, use meditation. This is the highest form for facilitating this growth and improvement. Yet, there are many others that can complement your improvement. Entering a dreamy mind space while creating something is an advancement in spiritual attention span. For instance, playing with paint or other art materials and just going where the flow is with it without any expectations of what you are creating will help you enter this space. Release the left brain's attempts to direct the project in any way.

Creatively visualizing in a relaxed state is another way to focus and an excellent one. Using sound vibration to change your atmosphere is another tool. This can be participating actively in making this music or merely listening to it on your own. There is much to choose from. Try chants, drumming, and ancient sounds for starters. Anything that makes you feel more energetic and happy is appropriate when it comes to choosing sound.

We are all constantly using our spiritual power and personal willpower toward either a negative or positive polarity. There is no medium point or mediocrity involved. By going within and examining yourself, including the payoffs and motives, you can know where you are coming from. Do not judge yourself, but just bring motives to your awareness for clarification and clearing where necessary. When oriented toward service to others and a positive polarity, you can feel good about your actions and efforts.

Knowingly or not, we are all trying to achieve a balance to live fulfilling lives. Your magical personality can be accessed and embraced during trying times as well. Often, when I experience something that shakes my world or jars me emotionally, I have typical feelings and responses at first. But I try to cut that short and not dwell in that space. I will then look at the challenge in front of me and actively seek what I can learn from it. How can it change or even enhance my life experience in the long run? Now, it may seem overwhelming,

but where is it going? How can I be open to what God Source or even my higher self wants to direct me toward with this? By being more curious about our circumstances, we do not have to totally embrace disasters but we can grow from them nonetheless in mind, body and spirit.

We cannot rely on outer conditions to feel good. When we cultivate a true, inspired goodness within ourselves, things around us begin to change. Again, it may not be instant, but it is a universal law and concept that I believe in. It is our emotional reactions to situations that dictate how we will handle trauma of any sort. In all situations, we can retain our personal God given power by choosing how we will react. By keeping this in our mind and activating our magical personality — drawing down the purer aspects of our higher selves, we help fuel a more beautiful, fulfilling life and world. We heal ourselves and ultimately others with this path and action.

Revisiting the words and experience I offered in Book I regarding cords between individuals, places, and things, realize that all is connected by these light strands including your connection to your higher self. As you draw down from that energetic cord between your human self and your higher self, this provides the knowledge and magical essence you are seeking. For reference, that information is contained in the chapter *Working With Energy in Book I.*

Notes – Thoughts – Ideas – Affirmations – Dreams

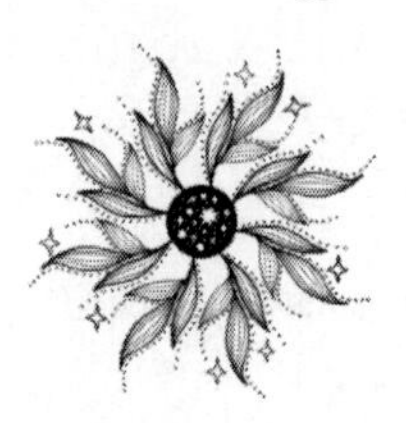

21 – Living Environment

"He is happiest, be he king or peasant, who finds peace in his home." ~ Johann Wolfgang von Goethe

The empath's personal living environment can be paramount to their emotional and physical stability in life. It is easy for it to be taken for granted. Yet, when elevated in the extreme importance it can hold, each empath will find it easier to live magically every day. As we explore this topic, I want to engage your imagination. You will be closing your eyes so if you are listening to the audio version of this book, perhaps skip this section and wait until you are in a place where you can be totally relaxed and able to close your eyes. If you can also grab something to write with — anything will do, that would be ideal.

For one moment, close your eyes and pretend you are a person with no knowledge of what an empath is, or a lightworker for that matter. You are meeting someone new for the first time. It could be anyone but let us pretend you are going to take a hands-on lesson of some sort from your higher self. You have heard this individual is a renowned teacher and you are to arrive at their home at 6pm.

As you arrive, what do you see? Close your eyes and imagine this person and their surroundings.

What does the exterior look like? Look at the entrance door. Is it just like any door on most homes? What does this person look like as they open the door to greet you?

Examine the interior as you step inside. What is the floor covering? Is there a color scheme? Are there things lying about and if so, what? What do you hear? Are there windows? If so, do they have drapes, shades or shutters?

How does this place smell? Would you consider the rooms dark or light filled? How do you feel in this area?

Does your teacher have any pets? If so, what are they like?

What types of items hang upon the walls, if any?

Go to the kitchen with your teacher to retrieve something. What is the kitchen like? Is it sleek and tidy or cluttered?

Are you finished imagining? Do you want to make a few notes as to not forget?

It is very likely that you have just conjured what you believe the personal surroundings of an empath should be like. It is very likely these elements you imagined mirror what you have now or would like to have in the near future. So, what are you waiting for? Let's get busy making your personal living environment that which you believe in and fulfills your expectations. First, we need to do a little mental and, most likely, physical clearing.

My husband does not like parting with things. In order to keep the peace, I have endured hanging onto things at our home that have been sitting around way too long. Worse, I realized that I had become like him as well. I cannot blame it on him. Perhaps, it is more of a fact of turning older. As we age and the prices of items we purchased in the past have risen significantly, we look at things we no longer need and say, "Wow, that costs a lot more now. I better hang on to this."

And, the cycle ensues. The problem with hanging onto items past the date we really need them is that they begin to pile up in closets, storage areas, garages, cupboards and shelves. I know. I hear you now. You are thinking, "yes, but I might need that someday." I realized it was way out of hand when my husband began collecting empty boxes. He felt that he may need that size box for "something".

Being able to say goodbye to clothing that no longer fits or you never really liked in the first place is a good starting point. Please do not feel sorry for the clothing. It will find a good landing spot. Nor should you feel bad for your sister that gave that to you … get rid of it. Donation sites for clothing and household goods are easy to find. If you want to make a new job for yourself (and that is what it can turn into), consider selling your items on sites such as Poshmark, Etsy, Ebay and more. There are also sites that will take your gently used clothing and sell them for you. Of course, most of the money they will earn as they photograph and house the items until they sell. You may find consignment shops for some of your items where they take a fee and sell the items for you. Take a long, hard look at this. Making room in your home can assist you in feeling like you can take a deep breath again and feel more relaxed. Go around your home and look in the closets and storage areas. What do you need to part with in order to have more breathing space?

Some of my husband's t-shirts are very sentimental to him from when he played in different bands around the USA. While they were faded or had tiny holes or rips (probably those darn groupies), I placed them in a plastic container with a lid and now store them at the top of the closet. Some items are worth saving for the nostalgia. Small things are especially easy to tuck into a special place or even make artwork from to hang on your wall.

Should we speak of garages? I didn't think so. In the United States, it would be wise to put two garages on each

home. One that you stack all your stuff that you may need someday into, along with real essentials and another one you can actually keep vehicles, bicycles, and such in. There — problem solved! But since most people are lucky if they have a home with a garage, we must be more practical about all this stuff we are saving.

People that have lived through lean, hard times such as the depression could not help but save everything. In fact, you do not have to experience a recession or depression in order to feel and live this way. Go without money or a job for awhile and you can be the same way. It is wise to be frugal, but it is unwise to pile up your environment with too many things you will never possibly even use.

We all know there are some things you are never going to part with until you are ready to check out from the planet permanently. For me, anything my children or grandchildren have given me has to stay. I cannot get rid of it … not yet anyway. When it comes to my crystals and gemstones, I may give some away if I want you to have it, but I won't part with them unwillingly. There are some things that are non-negotiable.

Let me be clear I am not suggesting that you throw everything out … unless you want to. I am just reminding you that periodically, you need to go through your living spaces and see what needs to be cleared. Everything is made of energy — everything picks up energy. What needs to go? One of the main reasons I suggest this is because we need to make room for the new things you will be manifesting into your life — even if that is just a clearer, more relaxing and beautiful space.

Once you have that accomplished … and I realize it could take awhile … time to jazz up the empathic abode.

When I was a real estate broker (which seems like a past life now), any home that had the right feel, smell and atmosphere when buyers walked in was going to sell and for

top price. Any home that did not was a struggle. Many homes stand out in my memory, yet one in particular took the top prize. The rooms and closets were not that large. The kitchen was not updated with the latest floor coverings, appliances or countertops. Yet, it was quite functional and pretty. The furniture was not new, in fact, it was quite old. But it was impeccable with finishing touches that adorned every room in a tasteful manner that was not too showy. It is hard to describe but if you visit or look at homes frequently, you will know right away. Overall, the house and property had a feeling of peace, comfort and being at home. There was a bidding war on who was going to own that property.

All humans respond to their environment and you can enjoy yours much more by paying attention to it and making it match your persona. Realize that style, comfort and peace are items you really cannot purchase. They are feelings and impressions. So, redecorating does not have to cost a lot or anything. Style is your personality showing through in the items that resonate with you. You build upon that theme and showcase your preferences in your home. Comfort is a feeling that can include the use of textures. Sometimes it is how things feel as you walk bare foot upon them. It could be the softness of throw pillows on the chair or couch. Comfort can be how a place smells. You may like to keep it smelling like apples and cinnamon are baking in the oven or you may want to keep a daily practice of perfuming your home in another way with incense. You might like a crisp lemon verbena scent in the air. All of this adds comfort to people.

Peace is achieved by having a calm atmosphere. It is not always achievable if you have a beloved pet that barks frequently or an overly excited toddler. But those are things you put up with because you love them and you learn not to allow them to interfere with your peace too much. However, things being out of place in a major way can create conflict visually and spatially. If you walk into a room and there are

piles of papers or empty boxes taking up space, this does not feel peaceful or comfortable. It feels like chaos and it is.

If you really need something fresh to excite you about your environment, begin with colors that make you sing. Wall paint is still relatively inexpensive and this can transform a room quickly. Then, thoughtfully add objects you actually need and love.

Sound - what sounds will fill your environment. Remember that the noises present can affect your peaceful feelings. Will the television(s) be on frequently? Do you have one person in your home that wants it that way and you do not? Make the most comfortable special area for them where they can indulge in this — even if it is a corner of one room. The point is that you can change the entire way your environment feels — thus changing the way you feel by paying attention and putting a little work into your surroundings. You do not need to spend money on purchasing new things. It is more likely that you need to sell or donate items to make your spaces inside your abode the way you want them.

By taking this loving approach to your living environment, you clear the way for new things to come into your life and you clear your mental space to be able to better facilitate manifestation which we will begin in the next chapter.

22 – Creating Your Future

"If you knew how powerful your thoughts were, you would never think a bad thought" ~ Unknown

Making things happen goes by many names. Some claim it all surrounds the law of attraction. Others claim it is just consciously creating reality. Always, the outcomes can be magical. On rare occasions and usually with divine intervention, I and many others have experienced miracles.

Manifesting and creating are not just buzz words that give humans hope. Our ability to attract things to us is part of our innate design. The Great Creator endowed us with this ability to co-create within our dimensional realm. This ability is ongoing and part of our design. It is not here when you catch it flying through the air and gone when you missed the ball. Here is the secret you may have realized but some have not: You are already manifesting all the time. Whether what you have manifested is considered good or bad, negative or positive is open for consideration and might be just a matter of perception. But, I know what you really want now that you are here. You want to know how you can more consciously direct it. That is what I aim to assist you with.

I have consciously created miraculous items and situations in my life such as finding the perfect mate for me, building my dream home, career goals, businesses, physical healing, money, and other things large and small. I have also

created (unconsciously) trouble in relationships, lack of money, jobs I hated, failed businesses, and health situations. I believe this puts me in a perfect position to teach what to do and not do.

What is required? An open mind will suffice. You don't have to believe what I am telling you. You just have to be open to trying it. This information is for anyone, not just empaths, who want something different! Maybe you already know how to consciously create your reality but you need a booster shot. You need someone to quickly remind you of how you have fallen off track. Perhaps you are new to the entire idea. You had the common misconception that your life is steered by fate, luck, or the "man". Fear not, you are about to be free from the self-imposed shackles on your legs and arms. No longer will you feel restricted as you work through these ideas and see for yourself what you can accomplish. Yes, you read that correctly. I did say "work". Yet, it will be the greatest gift you can give yourself and ultimately, others as well. The work will be experimental, fun and rewarding!

We are unconsciously or consciously manifesting and co-creating our reality on a constant basis. Humans who are not aware they are doing this or do not believe such a thing are still creating circumstances and things around them. For those that believe they have major influence over their lives and a primary role in it, often they fall into a couple of methods. We shall term this active manifesting and look at the two primary approaches seen most often with individuals, although there will be many variations.

The exciting possibility of being able to manifest money, relationships, achievements and more compels some to skip the self discovery journey and its subsequent transforming qualities. Generally speaking, they have some initial luck and do manifest some wonderful things. Often, this is followed by a period of being stuck and not able to attract their true desires as often as before. This can place them in a period of questioning

the entire manifesting process. Did they really manifest those things or was it just some strange luck? This period of time may also herald in a new beginning for the individual to look at their inner self closer and discover areas that need to grow. In this scenario, I have wondered at times if the higher self is not directing or controlling in some fashion to encourage the individual to do the soul work.

The second most common type of manifesting individual is one who totally believes in the law of attraction and all of its components, but is not using it effectively. This could be seen in that they may think of something they want to encounter or create, but put no further action or emotion behind it. They may not go to the trouble of visualizing it often or writing it down in an affirmative way. However, the main blockage for them is a worthiness factor. Somewhere in their minds, they are still grappling with a victim mode of thinking that is thwarting their abilities.

The percentage of people who are actually actively creating their reality on a consistent basis is probably fairly low. It is unknown, but I will guess that active creation is perhaps five percent of the population or less. Yet, it works for those doing so. It can also work for you.

My Introduction to Conscious Creation

I spent my teen years in the 1970's. Okay, I know you are jealous. Yes, it was truly an iconic era. I had been heavily involved in my church and started to feel disenchanted with the hypocrisy I saw there. My father had a few books on esoteric teachings. I do not remember what they all were but I know he had at least one on astrology. Over time, I dabbled in many subjects but seemed to settle heavily into astrology. By the time I was in my early twenties, I could prepare an astrological birth chart having taught myself the algebraic equations required for such. This is despite the fact that I was no math

whiz. I wanted to learn what made things tick for myself as an individual and to see the patterns in things with other people as well. I had memorized all the major influencing planets and their attributes, along with every sun sign's numerous traits. I would secretly guess a person's moon sign or rising ascendant based on their appearance or emotional responses. You can bet that if you were my friend or I had a relationship with you, I had already cast your chart.

However, it was not until sometime in the 1980's that I came across a book entitled *Creative Visualization* by Shakti Gawain. As I began to absorb the information in this small paperback, I realized that I had several obstacles to overcome. On one level, I believed every word of it. On another level, I was afraid of it. These fears stemmed from the religious teachings that had been ingrained into my mind. Was this dabbling in devious practices or was I being misled by the devil himself?

Unfortunately, it took me quite a few years to totally let go of these good vs. evil fears. Our brains are truly like computers and our belief systems are based on the information we have let in and the experiences we have endured. It was a valuable lesson in letting go of memories embedded into my brain cells. Often, I thought it was all gone, only to see it rear its ugly head in another form.

I do believe in a one powerful Creator God that constantly breathes us into existence and has given us this ability ourselves to co-create with it without limitations. It is our choice how we handle the gifts bestowed on the human entity as we were made in the image of the supreme creator.

During the late 80's and into the 1990's, I worked with the visualization process on many levels with different teachers and methods. I did create many things that were good for me and moved me forward in life. More lotus petals opened as I started to become self-aware and went through sometimes

agonizing hard looks at myself and my decisions of why I was stuck in certain jobs, relationships, or situations that were not good for me. I learned the number one lesson of my existence: personal responsibility

Personal Responsibility a/k/a Your Ability To Respond

The word "responsibility" can have so many negative connotations for us. I see my father when I hear that word and I hear him saying, "You have to learn to be responsible." Okay, what is that anyway? Live my life like you Dad? Go to college, get my degree, pay my bills on time, get old, sick and die? What is it to be responsible? As a teen or young person, you are either confused on what that means in its totality as presented by your parents or you are rejecting it because let's face it, it sounds like no fun!

One of my spiritual teachers turned me around on this when he taught: Responsibility is merely "your ability to respond". You decide how you are going to respond to things and why. This would include:

Any situations you find yourself in

Any decisions you have before you

When we phrase it as "how do I want to respond to this situation or decision", we have just turned the tables. We are now in control of it instead of being at the mercy of another. We all have the opportunity to take responsibility right now for:

- Our educational level
- Our finances
- Our relationships
- Our occupations or the way we spend our time
- Our habits
- Our health

- Our mood

It is easy to look at the list above and think that some people have no control over particular situations. Indeed, what fate hands us can be incredibly challenging. If we are born into a family of abusers, there is a point when we have the chance and the responsibility to break free from those family relationship ties. If we are born with particular health challenges, we may need to take responsibility (decide how to respond) so that we can still live a fulfilled life rather than blaming or questioning why it happened to us. If our finances are not what we would like them to be or completely messed up, who can change that? Only by taking responsibility are we in a position to permanently shift how we handle finances.

By taking responsibility — deciding how to respond — we take back our power. We recognize that we can make choices about what fate has dealt us and take control of our destiny by coming up with strategies and ways to respond to those people or events.

Basically, you have to come to a point where you never blame other people, circumstances or even the government for your plight that you perceive as challenged in some way. Instead, you must learn to play at this like life is a game and you want to choose how and where you will move your token on the board to advance. You realize that you will need to throw the dice to see how many spaces you can move at a time and that this is the chance factor. Yet, even that can be enhanced often in your favor.

Willingness to Bend

When you have a willingness to bend or make changes, this is part of being personally responsible. It means you see where you need to be different in order to achieve your outcome. This is something significant to consider because

many people may just want to believe they will imagine their desired outcome, yet do not see that they need to take some action to assist in setting up the circumstances where it could occur. These changes could be ways of thinking and focus or what you are willing to do or change. Here are some hypothetical examples:

Jane is always complaining that her hair is very dry and in bad condition. One of her desires is to have a beautiful, healthy head of hair that shines and is silky to the touch. So far, however, Jane only complains to her friends about her hair's condition. Many of her friends have made product recommendations but Jane nods and proceeds to ignore that information. She continues doing what she has always done with her hair. One day, Jane reads an in depth article about hair which explains how it is formed and many things she never considered. She learns that nutrition can play a large role in hair health along with regular brushing and the right hair products. Despite this, she still changes nothing about her nutrition or hair routine. Yet, she is still somehow expecting to have better hair.

It is almost like the universe is serving up the information to Jane about how to have the hair she wants. But, she refuses to make any changes. Do you know someone like this? Almost everyone does — always talking about what they are not content with. They often see the world as unfair. If they are gifted with something, they look for how the glass is half empty, instead of half full. Unfortunately, manifesting the true desires of these individuals is going to be tough. The reason is because they are more married to the idea they proclaim they want to be different. Fear is often involved if a change is needed. Many people are just more comfortable complaining about their situation than doing something to make a way for change to happen or things to manifest.

We all have to do our part. We have to open up an invisible hole in the fabric of our world that shows we are

willing to meet things even a small part of the way. By doing so, we are now open to receiving our desires. Try to make sure you are not doing that when it comes to your desires. If you find that you are, just forgive yourself and make a quick list of what you could do to be more proactive or make some easy changes first — harder ones later.

Desire

Speaking of what we want in this world, I remember when I was in my early twenties I made friends with a girl who I ended up spending quite a bit of time with. She had high ambitions for herself and, while I did not match her style of obtaining it, I remember a very poignant conversation we had. I was feeling somewhat guilty for having so many ambitious desires in life. I wanted so many things. She had grown up much more disadvantaged than I. In fact, she grew up on what she would call "the poor white trash wrong side of the tracks." She said I'll never go back to it. She was like a machine for an advertisement of the law of attraction. This is before anyone was writing books or having seminars on the law of attraction principles. If she wanted a new car, she would state what kind and color. She worked in sales so her income was unlimited — the more she sold, the more she made. A couple of months later, she would be driving that car. It was crazy and amazing and I felt lucky just hanging out and going places with her. Her energy literally felt like it rubbed off on me. Remember this empaths!

She and I had this conversation about whether it was "spiritual" to have desires for material things, certain people to come into our life, and other such things. We concluded after this long discussion that it was perfectly fine to have desires and that the Creator itself is built upon continual desires in the way it is constantly expanding and seeking experiences through the small particles it has created to accomplish such an awe

inspiring feat. If we stop desiring, we sort of lose the juice that keeps us excited and going in life.

Desire is what fuels the sperm to meet with the ova. It is part of the union of life experience that results in creation. In order to create or co-create with God/Goddess/All That Is, one must have desire. Additionally, do not try to take on your manifesting all by your lonesome. There is a reason it is called co-creating. You are essentially utilizing your emotions, beliefs and decisions combined with the all knowing power of God Force spirit to constantly create. When you feel overwhelmed, unsure of your direction or stifled in any manner, simply give it up to this God Force and ask for inspiration which is the pulling of spirit into one's self or being inspired (in spirit). When we are intuitively guided by this wonderful creator force, our lives unfold in a more harmonious way.

Notes – Thoughts – Ideas – Affirmations – Dreams

23 – Important Principles

"If you want to know the secrets of the universe, think in terms of energy, frequency and vibration" ~ Nikola Tesla

"**D**on't worry – Be Happy" so the song goes. These are simple words to sing but maybe not so easy to achieve day to day, moment by moment. You are going to have negative thoughts. It is inevitable. I have them and so does everyone else.

Allow me to tell you about an advanced spiritual yogi trick that will help cure this. You do not need years of training to do this. It is extremely simple. Each moment you catch yourself having doubts or negative thoughts such as "it will never happen to me" or "I am fooling myself with this nonsense", take the following quick action: Take a deep breath in through your nose and hold it for 10 seconds, then exhale through your mouth. No, really, are you alive still? Take a deep breath in, hold and notice that you cannot think negative when you do that. When your breath is at the top and you are holding it, your negativity is suspended. Notice how your chest and shoulders relax upon exhalation. When you are holding your breath, just imagine the negative feeling or thought to float out of your head. You may even visualize it encapsulated in its own dark little rain cloud, floating right off into the horizon. You could then replace it with a positive affirmation. The breath method works! Remember that point – your mind is creating your reality right now. Therefore it is of utmost importance that you listen to what is going on inside that gorgeous head of yours so you can make the proper adjustments.

When I began to consciously create my reality, mainstream science was not on board with these ideas. Unbeknownst to me, these principles were being heavily studied and applied at prestigious universities and many times in conjunction with our government. Princeton University began exploring the ways thought affects objects and matter in the 1970's and this continued through their Institute of Noetic Sciences. The NSA and CIA through Stanford University have conducted decades of research in this area widely known as "remote viewing". These are the known projects. There are many more conducted at top secret levels. Certainly, the Russians and China are involved with thought creation and control as well.

However, this information was not available to the general public and to some extent, is still not widely known. We are taught that life "happens" to us. Many of us become control freaks (okay yes I am guilty) trying to make sure bad things don't occur to us or our loved ones. We anxiously plan out our education, jobs, finances, believing that if we take the road that everyone says is safe, we will be alright. Yet, have you noticed those ideas don't work any longer? Maybe they never did. We have entered an era in the 21st century when everything that we thought used to work does not any longer. But that is another subject .... Let's get back to your new life!

A Quick List of How Your Thoughts Create Your Reality

Principle 1 – All is Energy

This fact is something you know but reminders of it are welcome because we can become so lost in the environment

surrounding us. Everything that you can see, hear, touch, taste, and feel is made up of atoms vibrating at different speeds. This includes water, light, sound, the rug under your feet, the rock in your pocket, your pet, your toes, or a bowl you eat your soup from. Absolutely everything when viewed at the molecular level is vibrating and moving and is subject to change ..... if desired.

Some items have a slower vibration and therefore more dense, like rock. Some items have a high vibrational speed and are more subject to change like water. Yet, even canyons are formed through the continual force of water. Water is a much lighter vibration and changes more easily than rock. It can be evaporated at the boiling point; frozen at the zero Celsius, or drank warm or cold between those two extremes.

There is also energy around us we cannot see that vibrates at a certain level. We cannot see radiation whether it comes from a medical device or an atomic bomb. Yet, in certain levels it is deadly to life forms. It too contains energy. We cannot see the infrared spectrum of electromagnetic radiation, yet we know it exists because we have invented devices that measure it and make it viewable. Your own body heat emits this infrared light because you are producing thermal radiation which is the movement of atoms.

Think of all the energy sources you cannot see or feel. The vibrating wavelength of your wifi service, microwaves from your oven, a radio station's wavelength, or your cellular service.

Absolutely everything seen or unseen is made of up energy. All around us we are experiencing vibrational frequencies that have the power to manifest in different degrees based upon their wavelength or speed. All of this energy has thus far in our scientific community only been measured as compared to the speed of light. Yet, there is something faster.

Principle 2 – Consciousness Drives Reality

As a child, I learned in school that nothing was faster than the speed of light. After being introduced to Shakti Gawain's book, I realized that she knew something different. Thought was faster and more profound than light. In fact, part of living in the light, was to master our thoughts.

Nothing (no thing) proceeds a thought. Before God said, "Let there be light", he had to think that idea. Thought is a lighter vibration form than sound or light and is therefore faster and more specific. You know that light has an effect on you and your world. You know that sound does as well. If you looked into the crystallized water studies by Emoto, you are aware that music has the ability to change the structure of water molecules. Yet, thought also affects all matter (Emoto, 2004).

Principle 3 – Attraction Laws

We have all heard like attracts like and opposites attract. Which is true? There is debate over this and let's try to break it down.

The principle of polarity from the Hermetic teachings states things may coexist that appear to be opposites but are located on the same frequency. Imagine a rod or pole where one end contains a very giving person and the other end contains a very selfish person. These two entities exist within the same pole but are exact opposites. Because they resonate in the same frequency band (or pole), they are alike in that respect. This is why we often find ourselves attracting someone who seems opposite, yet they are vibrating there on our same frequency band. We have to figure out why. In this particular situation, it is often because the selfless one needs to learn to be more selfish or self loving with boundaries. Ideally, the selfish individual would learn to be more giving. Their frequencies, while exact polar opposites, reside in the same area where they both have something to gain or learn if they choose to do so.

Contemplate the following fictional situation and answer the questions in your mind.

Lilah is not happy in her marriage. She feels ignored and that her husband, Derek, is selfish. She awakes many days ticked off with the situation and finds herself mentally nit-picking at his lack of organization and other faults she sees. She has done so much for him and this is how she is paid back.

Derek is beginning to think it is a no win situation with Lilah. She expects too much so he will just ignore her and hope she gets the message.

- What is Lilah focused on?
- What is Derek focused on?
- Are they focused on the third entity, the relationship?
- When it comes to their focus, are they continuing to create more division by holding that position?
- What could each of them do to shift things in a more positive direction?

This couple needs to find a way to meet in the middle (of the pole) to begin to heal the relationship. It will require some change on the parts of both to leave their extreme polarized attitudes behind and begin to move toward one another for solutions. If they do so, it will benefit them and the relationship greatly. Yet, do you see how they are alike and that like has attracted like? A lesson is held for each in this relationship. They are both suspended on the same pole or vibrational pit stop in space and time … with each resonating at opposite ends of the same pole.

Right now, you should be able to see from these three principles alone of reality creation how things work in greater detail. Remembering that all is energy, thoughts are very powerful and our situations that we do not like or bring us strife often have something to mirror to us and provide a lesson for soul and human personality growth.

24 - Money

"What we really want to do is what we are really meant to do. When we do what we are meant to do, money comes to us, doors open for us, we feel useful, and the work we do feels like play to us." ~ Julia Cameron

Money is one of the easiest things to manifest. We all have programs running inside our heads regarding money and these programs are attached to our deep seated, often hidden feelings about our personal worth. When I discovered my programs about money, it rocked my world. Because you see, I knew how to make money and how to withhold it from myself or be broke as well. I had to program my brain for a new way of looking at money — which is just another form of energy.

Quite a few years ago, I attended an online seminar about money and abundance. One of the most compelling questions I pondered while examining my attitudes about money was:

If your money was a person, what would that person look/be like?

Immediately, the following image came to mind: I saw a woman who looked wealthy, trying to convince everyone by day that she was well off financially. In reality, she had little money, large debt but dressed nice and said all the right things. If needed, she would borrow money to keep up this façade, thus accumulating more debt. But that was her by day. By

night, she was sitting on the sidewalk, slumped over and homeless. She was dirty, ugly and no one wanted her.

Once I saw this image, I knew how it totally reflected my programming from childhood. On the one hand, I was a first grandchild and an only child for the first thirteen years of my life. However, my mother regularly told me growing up, usually while hitting me, that I was nothing. "She wished I had never been born. I was nothing but a burden to her." She would then come to my room at night, cry at my bedside apologizing for her behavior and take me shopping the next day.

This revelation forced me to really look at what I did with money in my own life as an adult. I experienced problems with never having enough money even when I made a very lucrative amount each year. I did not save money. I spent and I allowed myself to never have that little rainy day fund despite the fact that I made plenty of money. Together, my husband and I both had a substantial income. But we were almost always broke. We were both self employed and when the lean months came, as they always do, nothing was saved back for those times. If I had saved, that would have been a sign that I truly valued myself. Instead, I did it all up like it was cocaine.

As you hear this, you are thinking that you don't feel sorry for me in the least. Nor do I. It was stupid, but it was my program of lack I was running. I could not see for the life of me that I was taking from that little girl who needed money (love) and letting her know she was worth having money by setting some aside for because she was valuable. She needed to know that she was loved, safe and worthy.

Instead, I constantly created a borrow from Peter to pay Paul scenario so that little girl could continue to feel unworthy, unloved, not good enough, etc. Oh, but I did take her shopping. Each time I had a real estate closing, I took her shopping at the mall or made some other elaborate purchase. I did this because I was telling myself I deserved it. I deserved it because I had

already blown through all the money from the previous closings (using the same methods) and had nothing to fall back on. Therefore, I had gone without and let my little girl suffer. Now, it was time to take her shopping after this abuse.

What a healing it is to see this old program running. What a relief to know it is only a program that can be reprogrammed and changed. But, how?

The first step was getting a really good idea of who this money person had been in my life. Obviously, she has one body, but two faces. In the daytime, she lived as a well to do woman putting on a false face of having not a care in the world and we see her "shopping" just like what would happen when my own mother felt bad about what had happened. Somehow, she is equating shopping with being valued, accepted and loved. By night, her shadow side kicks in. This is the woman with poor hunched over posture, sitting on the side of the curb, counting out what change she has left and wondering where her next meal is coming from. Where will she sleep? She is tired, old and ugly. She has no one to love her and she doesn't believe she is worth loving.

I needed a new person that I could put money on. My new relationship with money needed to be someone who loved me no matter what, who would never hurt me, turn on me, or tell me I did not deserve to live, no matter what I did. It also needed to be someone I could feel lots of love with. Who would it be or who was it already, waiting there at the side stage for me, someone who had possibly been there all along that I had ignored over and over again, breaking their heart.

I told myself to think deeply on this for a day or two. Something would happen, a dream, a remembering …. Something would happen to allow me to find my true money person. Within days, a wise, loving woman archetype began to emerge in my mind. It revealed someone who has traveled to the depths of her ridiculous past decisions and not been afraid

to look at her uglier sides. With that analysis, no matter how harsh it seemed at times, she forgave herself for all she did and did not do.

This wiser woman joined hands with the young girl child inside of her and spoke, “I will do everything I can to make you feel safe. I will make wise decisions and not be a spendthrift because you deserve to have stability. I will not take you shopping each time something good happens. But, I will set aside a reasonable portion of monies so that you will always have what you need. “

How do you handle this energy we use for exchange called money? If you were to imagine the money person inside of you, what would they look like? Imagine what they do on a daily and nightly basis — in public and alone. What does the face of this money person look like?

You see, money really is easy to manifest. Yet, it can make some people miserable if the programmed games they are playing with money energy are not in alignment with that person’s best interests. This is why it is always worth going over and examining because so many people believe that a good part of their happiness lies in how much money they have. Whether that is true or not is not the point. It is their belief they are carrying. So, let’s get this right. Learn who your money master or person is that is running the show and determine whether they are worthy to do so. Perhaps, we need to create a new money person in our mind to be the decision maker, the attractor, the saver and the investor.

Does This Really Work?

The answer is yes. In fact, you are already creating your future moment by moment. You may have not been doing it on a constant aware basis. Like many, you may be on auto-pilot with your thoughts and have attracted what you focus on the most and have deep emotional ties to for whatever reason. This is why so much work needs to be done on the inside, empath. I

want to emphasize that the transformation of you gives you the ability to focus with intent and generate the emotions necessary to create your reality. When you clear away those thoughts and situations that are not serving you, the path opens up for you to create new things and experiences that are based upon the higher point you are now resonating at. You are the key because this process goes on inside you. It is not an invisible cloud of energy outside of you that you learn to manipulate. The energy that brings forth your current reality is residing within you now.

That may feel heavy and like, Oh no. I can't just instantly change myself into someone who resonates like a millionaire. You are right. You cannot do it instantly, but it can be accomplished swifter than you may realize. Money is one of the easiest things to manifest and if you want a lot of it, no problem.

Let's explore this. If you wanted to go from being lower or middle class to becoming a millionaire, how could it happen and what could you do to spring it forward?

First, read books that teach you how millionaires think and make decisions such as *The Millionaire Next Door* by Thomas J. Stanley and William D. Danko or *The Millionaire Fastlane* by M.J. DeMarco. Study the biographies of millionaires you admire — not oligarchs. Begin putting forth the intention and write it down - I have a net worth of one million plus dollars.

How do you need to expand your understanding of money and how it works in this world? Millionaires must have significant personal knowledge when it comes to numbers, investing, finance and more. Continue or begin learning about these things in your spare time. A millionaire can hire an expert financial consultant, but to keep tabs on their money and grow it, the millionaire must have significant knowledge as well.

Otherwise, how will they know if someone is telling them the best course or not?

Next, what is the way you will make your money? Is it doing what you do now? If so, how do you need to level up to make that happen? If not, what types of changes need to be made to open that possibility for you? Is it too much work? Then, perhaps you don't really want to be a millionaire. You see, I happen to believe that if you are engaged in being paid for doing something you love to do and it fulfills a need others have, it all works out. You just have to find a way to do that different than the next person so that you have a unique offering to your future clients or customers.

Even if you do not love what you do or know what you would love doing, hope is not lost. If you still want to be a millionaire, continue to tell yourself that you are capable of it and somehow, it is going to happen for you. Then, leave it open and begin following clues as they pop up — small or large opportunities that arise. Perhaps you will marry someone who is a millionaire. Perhaps you will win the money through a lottery system. An unexpected inheritance could happen. Perhaps, you will suddenly invent something that everyone "has to have". Just leave it open and keep walking around and learning how to think like a millionaire by finding out how millionaires think.

I realize not everyone aspires to be a millionaire or accumulate more wealth than that. Yet in today's world, to retire with one or two million dollars means you can take good care of yourself into your senior years, give to others, and leave some for your loved ones when you pass on. It's really not the huge sum it used to be due to inflation.

Perhaps, you would like to just have all your bills paid and some money in savings each month added. If this is the case, this should be your manifesting goal.

Remember, money is easy to create. Money is not evil. The way one chooses to use it is on either end of the pole or in between – for positive or negative. Being wise with it takes education, thoughtful practice and effort.

Notes – Thoughts – Ideas – Affirmations – Dreams

25 – Levels of Belief

"Ask, and it shall be given you; seek, and ye shall find; knock, and it shall be opened unto ..." ~ Matthew 7:7 *The Holy Bible*

Do you have the power to shape your future? Not if you do not believe that you do. You will be blown around by the winds of fate and chance. Your ship has the capacity to move on a course toward your desired destination when you simply follow the tasks and gain the knowledge that holding onto false beliefs has cost you to date.

To begin determining outcomes and our destiny, we move from core feelings which are supported by a set of thoughts or even theory we hold about life. We can analyze our modus operandi by observation and reflection upon ourselves. It is revealed in the way we approach everything in our lives. It becomes a unique signature of our way of being and doing. In turn, this begins to generate what we attract or repel from us in our daily existence. If you can grasp that, by stepping back and viewing yourself from afar, you will come to precise "knowings" during these moments of reflection. This is where you can begin to make any corrections necessary to what is holding you back.

Self talk is composed of that little voice going on in your head that says, "You can never do that". "That will never happen." Many times, it is the voice we heard as a small child or during adolescence. Our thoughts are powerful forms of

vibration. While working with many victims of abuse, it has become very apparent to me that our thoughts must change at the level of the subconscious. This is difficult and challenging, but possible. Everyone on the planet battles with self-talk that is negative. Accept that fact and put the tools in place to quiet or retrain this area of your mind that is nothing more than a recorder of old negative information you have picked up somewhere.

Clearing deep ingrained patterns and beliefs that can inhibit your dreams is an essential step. This step is not one to run through quickly or ignore. In fact, this will be an ongoing exercise that you continually do throughout your life. Does this mean it will take you forever to manifest your desires? No, not at all. Often, you will begin to see things pop and happen for you swiftly after rethinking or removing just one or two patterns or beliefs. We see in the small things what needs to be corrected before we get to the big things.

What we feel we deserve is reflected in the smallest of ways we approach our daily and nightly existence. If we truly appreciate the little things in life and it shows by the way we conduct ourselves within what we call habits and behaviors, the things we attract to us really do reflect that.

You may be feeling like you have tried this law of attraction stuff before and it did not work out for you. You gave up. Here are some reasons you may have struggled to attract your desires:

Your level and quality of belief or doubt

Often, our past programming from a variety of sources since early childhood formed our beliefs surrounding what is possible for us and what is not. If those concepts are really not true, we have a voice in our heads telling us lies. This can go on for years and even an entire lifetime. It is time to really

examine thoughts that pop up in your mind regarding what you are worthy of and can achieve. Don't believe the programmed lies that some repeated to you because they were said to them. That does not make them true. You believing them fuels and possibly fulfills them. If you choose to not believe any longer and actively reprogram your subconscious, you will succeed in this.

Your Emotions

Our emotions could be seen as a gauge to measure where we are floating or resonating much of the time. In the chapter on *Emotions are the Key*, I go into more detail on how our feelings are the fuel for manifestation and reality creation. They truly affect our entire life and our inner self. Analyze what emotional state you are in the majority of the time. Being an empath, this is doubly important. Remember many of the techniques mentioned in Book I for instantly transmuting emotions that do not serve you by changing up the vibration around you. Also, review the poncho method and other tools to keep from absorbing the emotions of others that you do not wish to have.

Clear Understanding of the Laws

By having a very thorough understanding of the dynamics set up with the laws surrounding manifestation and creation, you will experience more success. These laws are simple, but can seem complex due to old patterns of learning we have all experienced that turns these concepts on their heads. Keep learning and growing as a result.

Discipline

Many just fall out of the regular practice of using the concepts they have learned. It is very easy to have this happen because we live busy lives and often have put our doing as a priority over our imagining. It is probably more important to spend 15 or 30 minutes a day working on your manifestation desires than many other tasks you are engaged in. Make the time and space for yourself and you will surely begin to see quick results.

Failure to Launch

Have you ever missed an opportunity due to some sort of hesitancy that you felt? If we do not take action when the universe is trying to respond to our desires, we can set ourselves back on the reality creation wheel. I believe that often a similar or the same opportunity can come around again, but it could be awhile. Most of the time, this happens because we feel some fear. We feel confused and are not sure if we should take the leap or not. Learn to use your intuitive skills to assist with this. If you read runes, oracle cards or practice some form of divination, this can be a good way to ask is this the right thing for me or not when you feel unsure. You may just simply check in with your body and ask if it feels right or not. Take small moments being deep and reflective on the question. Examine yourself and the situation to come to an answer.

Desired outcome not being optimal and/or infringing upon the free will of others

Being too exact - I want _____ to love me and only him or her. Something may be in the background waiting to appear for you that is much greater and more ideal for you than you can imagine yourself. Plus, the person you have named may have other plans and you are infringing upon that whether you

use magic law of attraction or a magic charm potion on them. Everything must come together from a point where all have free will to choose their destiny. As many of you have learned, keep your desires you want to manifest open ended and in the present tense as already happened. Use statements such as:

"The perfect lover is entering my life now. I am open to experiencing deep bonds of love with this person."

"My company has found the exact mentors, employees and clients to succeed. This or something greater is happening for me now."

Having Trust

We have all heard it said that if you knew you would succeed; or, if you knew you would be supported, what would you do? Would you follow through on your desires based upon the solid, balanced belief that you will be supported? If your answer is yes, this is trusting your path. On this path of manifesting your destiny, our trust can be interrupted numerous times. It happens to all of us. Something throws us off balance. It is then that we must use our heart to feel where and how to get back on the path and regain our knowing, our belief, that all is progressing along. Many want to see the final results before they even get a few hundred feet down the pathway. Keep moving and keep believing. Remove doubt where you can and you will be on your way to achieving all you desire on the road to manifestation or something greater.

Feeling Stuck

Many times on the path of manifestation, we are beginning to leave where we were in the original situation and we are sort of stuck for a time before the new manifestation has actually become real and apparent to us. It is at this time that most people give up on their desired outcome they have been

holding in their mind's eye. This is the time to double down with your level of belief. What you want or something you love even more lies just on the other side of this time period of walking between two points of time. Know that it will make itself visible within the perfect time and space just for you. Yes, just for you. If you have not done so already, make some type of visual to reinforce your desire. This could be a vision board, drawings in a sketchbook, magazine cutouts on your refrigerator, a Pinterest board or a screen saver on your computer. Trust this time of having planted your seeds but not yet seen the fruition. Keep firm in your belief!

Affirmations

How and why do affirmations work? First, by reciting them often (as in daily) out loud or in your mind, you are reprogramming your subconscious where many of your base beliefs are stored. Many of the ideas you have stored there began in very early childhood, even as an infant. What happens when you start loading up this dusty library area of the brain with newer positive messages? Sometimes, a war ensues because the old data in the library is saying, "hey wait a minute, this cannot be true. If that is true then I no longer exist as an idea." You will see this come out in strange ways in your outer life as you are challenged to rethink things. The best thing to do is to continue with affirming the new positive thoughts.

However, you want to ensure that the affirmations being used are believable to the ego portion of your brain. Otherwise, it will not take hold or at least experience severe delay in delivering the change in beliefs and attitudes you are striving for. An example would be:

Possibly Unbelievable Affirmation:

I am wealthy right here and now and have more money in my bank account than I could ever spend.

What is right about the above affirmation is that it is written in the present tense — happening now. However, it may be too much of a stretch for your ego to believe.

Another Unbelievable Affirmation:

This Saturday, I will win the lottery and be a multi-millionaire.

Here, we have two things wrong with the affirmation. One it is written in the future instead of the present. Affirmations to be their most effective should be in the present moment. They also need to be a little more general than limiting your ways of obtaining wealth only to winning the lottery. This is too controlling on the side of free will and does not allow for things to come the way they need to you in the perfect time/space sequence.

Better Believable Affirmation:

Wealth comes to me in so many different forms each day, including money. Everything I need comes to me in the perfect time and space. I am prosperous.

This affirmation is written in the present moment and can be used each day. Notice how there is no lack involved as all that is needed comes with perfect timing. It indicates that wealth includes more than just money because it does. Often, we receive prosperous value in other forms such as something free; deep discount on something we wanted or needed; a sudden large order or numerous orders for items you may sell or services you provide; an incredible opportunity to be included with others in a marketing or money-making

opportunity. Prosperity can also be viewed as priceless moments with loved ones and friends. All of these, including money, make for a well rounded, fulfilling prosperity that you can take to the bank of life.

Some people complain they forget to state their affirmations. This really comes down to habits. However, there are visual tools you can use to remind yourself as well as other techniques. If you drive somewhere each day, you can make a recording of your specific affirmations on your phone and play it as you begin your way in the vehicle. A great visual reminder is perhaps a pendant, necklace or bracelet that is your visual cue to state your affirmations. You could select jewelry items that have specific messages engraved upon it — such as self-love - faith - believe. I kept a small sign on the back of the bedroom door that said "Believe". Each time I closed the door, it was my reminder if I had not practiced my affirmations that day. Additionally, it came to serve as its own unique bundled message. After some time, all I had to do was see the plaque and I was able to invoke the positive feelings immediately. I still use the sign, but in a different area now .... my office.

26 – Carpe Diem

"*Abundance is not something we acquire. It is something we tap into.*" ~ Wayne Dyer

When you have sufficiently retrained your brain with affirmations and have begun to see the miracles large and small that pop up now in your life, you learn to trust. By staying with your practices and keeping your emotional state as steady as possible, things are beginning to smooth out for you. Now, you know that law of attraction, creative visualization and manifesting do work. However, you wish you felt more control over it and could do it more of the time.

You are similar to a Rookie of the Year player who has practiced and followed the advice of your coaches to the best of your ability. It's for sure, your skill is on the rise and that is why you were named the best new player of the year. However, you have to level up from here. Rookie status is ending as new athletes enter into their first years. To progress toward a seasoned player, you must continue everything you have learned, continue training, and add some new exercises along the way.

For the most part, we are working with the same tools or ingredients. As you travel along the manifestation path, you may add a new one here or there. These are usually methods that work as supporting features in your arsenal of tools to create reality. A couple of examples would be a computerized

application that reminds you of certain things or a vision board. The one tool you must keep as sharp and ready as possible is your intuition. But don't keep that tool hidden in the drawer. Combine it with your ability to hear it and feel confident about following its urgings. So often, we believe in our logical mind that we know what we want. Sometimes, a higher part of us knows the real answer and where we can finally hit pay dirt or treasure. By allowing intuition to lead, we walk a more graceful path toward the reality we want to create, even if there are dead ends or forks in the road at times. By trusting this part of us, we will quickly pass anything that might initially seem like a stop sign or hurdle.

The A-Frame

Early in our marriage, my husband and I bought a piece of land and believed that we wanted to build an A-frame home on it. In fact, my husband drew up the plans and we had much time, visualization and emotional energy into this. More than anything, we wanted to build a house. We did not have the money, or income at the beginning to justify such a thing but it was our dream that we continued to nurture in a positive way.

A couple of years later, I broke my right thumb when I took a tumble on a wet floor and tried to catch myself with it. Suddenly, it put me out of commission to do the computer legal work I was performing for a couple of attorneys in town. Money was getting tight for us on my husband's income only and before I went to sleep one night, I prayed with a lot of emotion and took my burdens to God. I asked that I be shown what I could do to remedy this situation while I was still in a cast that covered most of my hand. That night, I had an extremely vivid dream about me driving a blue SUV. I had a briefcase with me and other things I did not currently own. I was selling real estate and I felt extremely happy in the dream — like it was my optimal career. I woke up early, put on coffee

and felt very excited. When my husband woke I said, "Guess what honey, I'm going to sell real estate." By the end of the day I was enrolled in school for same and it became a thirteen year career in which I not only helped other people make their desires come to fruition, but my own as well. Here is something important to tell you and then I will get to the A-Frame house. I never wanted to sell real estate prior to that dream — never! My mother had been a real estate agent and I absolutely abhorred the idea of it. She often came home with nightmare stories. There seemed to be a lot of stress. She never received a paycheck unless she went to a closing. I wanted no part of it. But, something happened that night in the dream. It was very vivid and real. Moreover, the extreme happiness I felt doing the job allowed me to know that I needed to follow this cue. I had asked God and the answer was instantly delivered.

Selling real estate in a new state where I had moved when marrying was challenging at first. I did not know many of the roads or any people to speak of. I really had to put myself into it and work hard and smart. Of course, I brought my skills at attracting the right things into my life knowingly and unknowingly. One of the things I first attracted was a new listing I took on 27 acres at the edge of the county. It was an A-Frame home. Suddenly, I was now able to see what one of these homes was really like from the inside. Due to the slope of the ceiling on each side, furniture placement was difficult — especially upstairs. Unless there was a straight physical wall in the main level before the roof began to pitch so severely, all furniture would need to be situated in the center of the living room. I pointed this out to my husband and he made some changes to the blueprint drawing he had been creating.

As the property was shown to many prospective buyers, it became clear that people were attracted to the A-Frame style and wanted to look at it, but actually buying it was another thing. Each buyer seemed dumbfounded on how to make the inside of the home work well for their lifestyle. I learned through my more experienced agents at the office that A-Frames sit on the market a long time generally before they sell. Sharing this information with my husband, another dream home style began to form in our minds — one which finally was built.

Let's dissect this shortened version of the longer story. First, something that could be considered bad led me to an occupation I thrived in and loved. Without that occupation, I do not know if a way would have been opened for us to make a huge jump and build our house. The breaking of the thumb and the turmoil over money led me to pray and ask for guidance. Notice — I asked! That's a key component to getting divine assistance.

Once the dream was given to me, I acted right away upon it. I did not hesitate to find a way to make it happen. It was not all smooth. I had to put out effort, but I grew and learned more from it. I also was gifted with an A=Frame listing in the very beginning by chance (or not). This allowed me to know that the house style may not be the best decision for us. Despite the fact that we had imagined this home style in our minds and my husband had committed to it with hours of work on paper at night after his regular job, the universe was hinting and allowing us to know it would be better to change this aspect of our desired outcome.

When you determine things are not coming to you as you desired/expected, you might want to rethink it. A bad or undesirable thing happening can lead to good solutions for short and long term. What you thought you wanted may need to take a little detour to get there. Plus, the universe may have something better to offer than that which you originally desired.

Listen to your dreams and intuition. It will be clear to you — not vague. Act and follow the direction even if it seems impulsive or crazy — as long as you are being legal and safe.

Live with a mindset of seizing the day — not a day in the future, but today. There are several ways to do this and the most important method will be mentioned last. It is a major key that unlocks the ability to be a master manifestor. Truly, if we do not back up our desires with action when an opportunity is presented, we set back our ability to manifest what we have been wanting and dreaming of.

Fear is what holds people back. Remember the acronym for F-E-A-R = False Evidence Appearing Real

You must be willing to act when you are moved emotionally toward something or when a possible connection or situation is presented to you. Let us analyze each of these levels of wanting:

Levels of Desire

I have seen people almost instantly manifest material things, connections with others, or situations that bring them closer to a goal simply by thinking of it, but letting it go very quickly and without deep emotional attachment. As I have viewed this, I wondered if these are instances where the individual is a gifted manifesting machine. That conclusion is possible. Yet, I believe it is more probable this is a human state we all can naturally achieve when other things are not hampering it — especially where the emotions of the individual are concerned. It is very possible that our emotional states, which reflect deeply held beliefs, color what is possible for us and what is not.

Another person may obsess with their thoughts, visualizations and outward actions to attract the same situations

or even larger ones and this works for them. This perceived extra effort is then viewed as what it takes for them to manifest. However, could it be that it is merely an unidentifiable point in time and space of where we are resonating? That is the main question to be explored.

I believe there is another way to do this that brings the results you want and need. You may say to yourself that you have creatively visualized, cut out photos, and threw in a few cartwheels to ask for what you want. The key is on the receiving end of this. Yes, the asking or desire must be an intention held to begin with, but then you receive by:

- Stepping Into It
- Believing It
- Owning It
- Being It

Your ability to imagine what you want and believe it is achievable covers the first two steps. Next, you must feel yourself owning it in some way. Finally, you are actually being it.

All desires must be viewed in the mind's eye or said out loud with affirmations as if they already exist. If you are writing your desired manifestations down anywhere — make sure it is in the present tense as already happened.

The reason is simple. If you are constantly thinking about something you want in the future — that's where it stays. By bringing it right into your NOW, you summon all the forces to make this happen. Essentially, when we believe we do not have something yet, we are playing in the lack paradigm. The anticipation of it just keeps it somewhere swimming around in front of us, but never within our true grasp. We are not focused in the now feeling like we are truly capable of being, having what we want. Moreover, we are lavishing our dreams into tomorrow.

Vibration matching is an advanced technique, but one easy enough for beginners. We have all heard the expressions, "Walk the walk and talk the talk." And "Fake it until you make it." Ironically, pretending something is a certain way when it is not can be a very effective manifestation tool. Many worry it will seem like they are not living their "truth". But, isn't it your eventual truth? Take a chance and step into being the person who would be experiencing what you want to manifest. Step into the role even if it seems delusional at times. This will bring you closer to your desired outcome.

Be what you desire. If you want to be a high paid nanny, the head of a successful company, a rock star, motivational speaker, famous athlete or some other public figure, you need to begin acting like you already are. This is an old, but true, way to assist greatly in becoming what you want to be. The saying, "walk the walk and talk the talk" comes to mind. The fact is — no matter how you want your persona to be, you must begin by acting like you own it now. If you want to be a dedicated husband and father, the role has a certain flavor and vibration. If you want to be a successful entrepreneur, this too carries outer and inner clues. Begin thinking and acting like you already are.

Be a dreamer, yet also a doer. Put the action behind your desires. Actively daydream your wondrous reality into existence. Everything is possible! Step into your destiny by figuring out this: What does my desire look and feel like? If I suddenly were already having my heart's desire, how would I be different or would I at all? Once you have determined that, begin operating as if it has already occurred. Look like that. Feel like that. Be like that.

Notes – Thoughts – Ideas – Affirmations – Dreams

27 – Being Bountiful

"If you approach the ocean with a cup, you can only take away a cupful. If you approach it with a bucket, you can take away a bucketful." ~ Ramana Maharshi

We all deserve a bountiful life filled with plenty. We must move from lack thinking by being mindful of our habits and patterns. This can include habitual ways of relating, living and the thoughts we think. It is important to recognize how our negative ego and ingrained patterns of thinking are expressing lack in our lives. We have to ask ourselves, how did these patterns become part of me? Many times, they are passed onto us by our family of origin and some people believe that certain emotional patterns that have a trauma causal factor can be generational. In other words, the pattern has been passed on via DNA. If so, more aggressive clearing techniques should be employed to remove these limiting ways of living.

When one or more individuals strike out to change the family dynamics, this provides a clearing for others in the line of lineage going forward. This is just one way of many that reveals when we heal ourselves, we do help heal the world. As we break chains that may have held the family in some sort of restrictive state with particular patterns, it frees everyone going forward if they choose.

Patterns can affect us all or part of the time. When they just surface periodically, this can be why we are a bit on and off with our manifesting abilities. The more you know yourself within and transmute your thoughts, the more you will experience the good things you desire.

Many times, we think too small. “Oh, I just need enough for myself over here in this corner.” Why not go bigger? If it does not happen, you do not have to be disappointed. It is likely you will have progressed a little more than just staying in your corner of the world. Why not have a bigger bounty, as long as you are comfortable managing it?

How can we recognize when we are holding back the good we deserve? It can often show up as indecision which is really just a fear of making a choice. Lack mentality also shows up as being in some holding pattern where no choice is being made about something or no action taken. When this is happening, it is because fear lies at the bottom of it all and the person does not trust making a move. On the outside, this can look like procrastination.

Lack shows itself when you think or openly state that you will not get enough. The fear that underlies here is that your needs won’t be met. Why? Who did not meet your needs in the past?

A feeling or declaration of giving up can be rooted in fear and lack thinking. After making the claim that you have done all you can do and now you cannot do anything else, you stay hooked to the situation by consistently focusing in a negative way in the situation or person of the past.

Often, we produce anxiety and fear over doing new things that are out of our comfort zone. It is important to push ourselves at times to try new situations. Otherwise, we can stay in a rut which is really just another position for lack and we cannot grow and manifest well in that state.

In the previous section, we found out that a major key or secret to being a master manifestor is to just step into what you desire like it already has happened or exists. Now, I want to provide some real life examples of why this can be challenging and then, what to do about it. This is the second key to hold and know about this subject. It relates to your openness to have and receive — to feelings of being worthy for sure, but also being a vibrational match up.

Let's say you want to increase your present income by fifty percent which is basically one and a half times what you make now. Who at the company you work for or with is currently making that amount of money? Is there more than one person doing it and if so look at a few of them and determine: How are they accomplishing it? What are the differences between the workload, clients, or personnel they handle compared to what you presently do? What else is different in their approach to their career? Do they have any specialized knowledge or education that qualified them for that position?

Once you have sat down with paper and answered these questions, look at it all again and ask these questions. Would you really be comfortable performing the tasks and working to meet the requirements that are necessary at that level? If so, great. If not, then perhaps there is another way open for you to boost your yearly income.

To go through the detailed whys of what you want in your mind is an important part. You may know someone who says I want a new Tesla and a one million dollar condominium located in a beautiful area where I do not have to mow the grass. Oh, and I want plenty of money to pay for my lifestyle. If the person wishing this already has net assets of around a million, perhaps a little less, this is not a large stretch for them to manifest. But, if they are making minimum wage or slightly above and want to make this leap, it will be extremely difficult to manifest, but not impossible. The reason is multi-fold and I hope you see from this chart below why:

Manifesting Goal

Wants new Tesla & Million Dollar Condo

Plus Enough Money to live comfortably with lifestyle

Minimum Wage Earner **Person with Value of $800,000**

Minimum Wage Earner	Person with Value of $800,000
Not enough income Creates stress & worry	Feels financially secure Money is not an issue
Has doubts about making substantial money	Feels confident about making or receiving more money

With the above example, it is such a great jump to make for the minimum wage earner that it is quite challenging for them to step into the Tesla/Condo lifestyle they desire. However, it could happen if they inherited or won a large sum of money. Would the law of attraction or reality creation have played a part in that? It is very likely it would. Can this individual actively use their imagination each day to go through life pretending they already have this outcome or better? That is the big question.

Each time they get behind the wheel of their current vehicle, can they see themselves actually driving their new Tesla? When this person arrives home, will they waltz into their current abode or for fun often pretend they are walking into that gorgeous home with its wall of windows overlooking the prized area they want to live around?

What happens if they spend time pretending they already have what they want? It transforms and changes their energy! But, they need to perform it with enthusiasm. They must also forget the fact it is not in front of them now.

Emotional pretending is a large key to this. Having faith and knowing that or something even better is coming your way.

For the person who has achieved a large net worth to date, the move to driving a Tesla, living in the condo, etcetera, is not a pipe dream to them. They are going to see it as achievable and could actively begin visualizing all of this with a greater realism perhaps than someone monetarily further away from it.

If you are a performer or in a band, are you going to take the stage like you are just a little local guy or gal that has not hit the big time yet? Or are you going to come out as a performer, an artist, giving it your all and being your best. That's what the audience wants. They want your energy to come through and they will give it back. It's a reciprocal thing just like all things in the universe.

If I came to meet you right now and put you in a box and declare to others: This is ____ and this is what you get when you open the package. I would go on to describe your wants, needs, desires, fears, energy level, tendencies, habits, core beliefs, what you do daily, goals, dreams, unhealed wounds, and best traits. Here you are in one package and this is the you that is the manifestor. It is not just the you that thinks positive thoughts, creates a vision board or writes your goals in a book. These are all important reinforcing items. They are sort of like things you do to seal the deal even more, but they are lower on the important scale than what you are in that package.

The box you are in — that really you have unknowingly placed yourself in — is where you resonate. While it may vary in vibration a little from here to there, it stays mostly at a certain frequency. If what you are wanting is a large jump in frequency, you must find a way to raise your vibration — change what's in the box to come into alignment with it and be a match.

Many people do fake it until they make it. They will accept no other reality in their mind. If they believe they are going to be a world great guitarist, playwright or space astronaut, they accept no other outcome in their world. They fake it by placing themselves constantly around others involved in the same thing, learning from them. They fake it by walking down the road a little different from most with their knowing that they are going to succeed in their endeavor. They figure out what those who achieved their dream did that they are not doing. While it might seem like this is all play acting and based in fantasy thinking, it is a major key to bringing it into reality. You are building it on a mental level, pretending it exists on a physical level and going through the motions to back it all up.

Let's say you want to manifest a permanent, fulfilling relationship. What do you need to do in order to achieve this? First, to have a clearer picture in your mind of what you want, look not to Hollywood movies, but to real successful long term relationships. What are these individuals doing? How do they interact with one another? How did they meet and what was going on with them each individually when they did hook up? Then, begin putting forth a vision for what your ideal relationship would be like. Leave the other person faceless/nameless. If you are trying to mentally force someone you know to be with you in that way, this is a clear indication that you are not on the magical path, but on one that leads to heartache. This is infringing upon their free will.

Once you know the type of person you want to be in a relationship with, begin imaging who they would be attracted to and what they might look for in a mate. Do you see that in yourself now? Do you need to make some changes or spruce up a little to begin to resonate at the same frequency this other person resonates at?

In today's reading world, many like to read books where the protagonist meets a billionaire and they live happily ever after at some point. In the real world, billionaires do not

come across too many of people they fall in love with that is their secretary or tailor. When they do, there is often some distortion or disconnect from the differences in societal structures these two are accustomed to. The billionaire is not better than the other person … I am not suggesting that. They are just different people coming from two different worlds — resonating differently. For the average person to suddenly seem romantically long term exciting to the billionaire, that person must match in some ways — resonate the same at some level for things to work out long term.

Rich people think rich thoughts and act differently than people who are worried about money. People in successful long term relationships think different thoughts and act differently than those who have recently split up with someone or are single.

Now, I am going to tell you something else important. All rules are meant to be broken. Ever heard that before? Of course, you have and this one is no different. There are a limited amount of people that can actually just have enough belief and skill at thinking intently about what they want to bring it to fruition even though they may not resonate there yet. I cannot tell you who those people are or what their exact qualifications are to do this, but, they exist. Keep this in mind as you could be one of them. How will you know?

Look at your past and ask yourself if you have ever wanted something pretty bad, daydreamed of it and then, boom — you got it. If so, you have this skill within yourself still. Perhaps you have just not exercised it recently. Skills can become dull when we do not continue to use them. Or, perhaps you had something occur that shocked your world — something sudden that tilted your core belief system. This could also put a damper on such a natural ability.

Envy, Jealousy and other Lower Emotions

Whenever we believe the grass is greener on the other side, we are not valuing what is currently around us. This locks us into a lack paradigm. Perhaps we have slipped into feelings of dissatisfaction. Often, this can spiral into envy of what others hold. Always, this is just the negative ego portion of one's self rising to the surface. As it shows its ugly teeth and roars, do not allow it to get its claws into you. It is time to tame this beast by letting it know all is well with everything around you.

Having what others have will not bring you happiness. That is a mind game of lack wherein we are tricked into thinking that way. By appreciating the blessings in our life, we attract more of what suits us. What others have or hold may not be the best highest thing for us. Besides, the more we covet what another has or their position in life, the more dissatisfaction we feel in our own world.

Your energy field will brighten and change as you live more in the moment appreciating all the wonderful things you already have in front of you. This breaks the cycle of lack thoughts. It also begins to set up an attraction situation for abundance in your life. So, feed that gratitude daily. Allow others to have their experience and bless them for it. If they can achieve that, you can achieve that or something better too. Most likely, it will be something you love even more.

May all be abundantly blessed and experience being bountiful.

28 – Gift Is The Shift

"Gratitude is the healthiest of all human emotions. The more you express gratitude for what you have, the more likely you will have even more to express gratitude for." ~ Zig Ziglar

Some days it is more challenging to feel gratitude. There are many situations in life that can clog our energy vibrational signature and have us feeling differently. Yet, your energy or vibrational signature can attract many, if not most, circumstances you find yourself in. This can include people you attract and things that manifest in your daily life. Some people read that and immediately think, "Yes, but what about ______? I did not attract that." I have said the same things at different times in my life. Yet, when I really analyzed the situation prior to the event happening, I believe I did. By taking personal responsibility for where I was vibrationally resonating prior to the event, I can see how if I was different — the event would have been mitigated or would not have happened at all.

What creates our vibrational signature? First, it is good to know that the signature is always shifting and changing. It has the capacity to totally transform into something other than what it was at any given moment. This happens via the intensity of the thought patterns and charged emotions within our mind/body/spirit complex. Now, to a degree, you have an overall spiritual vibrational signature that you currently carry — that you came into this world with. However, even that can change depending upon those same elements — thoughts and feelings.

You may ask yourself: "what about all this spiritual knowledge I have accumulated? Does it change my vibrational signature, hopefully advancing it toward the positive?" It could and often does. Yet, you must ask, "How do I use that knowledge? At this point, knowledge has condensed itself into thoughts and beliefs you have adopted. Those thoughts and beliefs could be helping or hindering you. Only you know which is the probability or truth. If you are like most humans, some are holding you back and some are advancing you. How can you analyze this and know for sure? Look to your emotions surrounding different subject matter.

Clearing Techniques To Improve Your Vibrational Energetic Signature

Ultimately, if we regularly work on knowing self and clearing residual energy away that is not in our highest interest, we will be more successful in steering our life toward the beautiful destinies we desire. Clearing Your Energy can often come down to simple practices by using physical and mental techniques that have been used for centuries. While the physical ones can be the most pleasant and health rewarding, working on clearing away negatively mentally is just as powerful. Let us look at possible ways to achieve the clearing away of negative or unproductive energy.

Physical Activities

- Tai Chi or Qi Gong
- Yoga
- Smudging
- Breath Work

Color Breathing

Remembering that each and every color and shade is composed of vibration itself and waves of light. Our entire universe is vibration and waves of light. Each shade or color has the capacity to produce a particular emotion to have an effect as it blends with us. If you know you are low on physical energy, you may want to experiment with breathing in the beautiful shades of red that exist. If you are anxious or jittery, try a cool ice blue. Is there red hot anger coming off of you? Tone it down with beautiful rich plant and forest shades of green. You can practice breathing in a particular color any time of the day to change your mood. If you have trouble at first visualizing a color, visit a store that offers paint samples and pull a few in every range of color you feel you need to focus upon. Use those color chips to assist you as you close your eyes and visualize deeply breathing in the color.

The entire technique is very simple. Sit or lie comfortably with your legs and feet uncrossed. Slowly breathe in the color through your nose. Hold the breath for just a few seconds — not any longer than what is comfortable. Then fully exhale the color through your mouth. In through the nose, out through the mouth. Visualize yourself in a bubble or cloud of the desired color

Mental Activities

- Meditation
- Creatively visualization
- Walking Meditation in Nature
- Chakra Balancing Meditation

Mind Dumping in Journal

When I have things bothering me, especially in the morning, I often will grab a notebook and just begin writing about everything that comes to mind. I pay no attention to

spelling, grammar or sentence structure. You can mix this also with drawings if you desire. I may write one page, but more often approximately three as I break down everything that is eating at me. The subject matter could be something another is doing that is grating on my nerves or a true betrayal of some type. It could be me sounding off about anything in the world that disturbs me, like human trafficking. Another thing that is great to mind dump on is when you feel insecure, not enough and allowing those thoughts to escape to the paper. Once it is completed, keep it for a little while if you want. You will grow past the place you are right now in most cases or you will begin to think of solutions (things you can actively do) to cope with what was bothering you. As a writer, I may put together a free pamphlet or ebook for parents on how to keep children and teens safe from predators.

Your Core Self

One morning, I awoke and decided that one of my aims to fulfill with the rest of my life was to become more and more magical each day. One way or another, I would express, impress, absorb and transform into the magic around me each and every day or night. This was an important step for me because, in it, I realized the magic of immortality. I realized that my magic would extend into all the edges of everything like a bright color bleeding into the sunset. Nothing was going to dampen or take my magic — not the strife of this world … or the next.

Ultimately, we attract from where our vibration is resonating. It's hard to always believe this statement …. But it is true. When we are operating in a world model of lack and limitations, our projected experience serves up those situations for us. What the true self holds at its very core is something to continually reflect upon. Here are some subjects to examine when doing this:

Am I a giving person or afraid it will not be appreciated or reciprocated?

Do I forgive myself easily and often? What about others? Remember forgiving others is one thing and tolerating continual bad behavior from someone is another. This would fall into the category of boundaries.

Are you being genuine or tricking yourself? In other words, do your thoughts and actions match what you claim to be? For instance, you may believe that all people have value and sparks of creativity. What do you find yourself thinking about those who you do not get along with; who are homeless; who are criminals? Do you really believe that? If you don't, just acknowledge it and be genuine with yourself. A genuine thought or statement could be: "I want to see the value and creativity inherent in all people, but sometimes I struggle with some." When you make this shift, it is toward a place of being more real and this clears your vibration toward truth. This shift in your statement about what you believe will also assist you in beginning to see the value of others that rub you the wrong way so that you eventually will be more like the original, higher thought you claimed to have.

Do you feel worthy of all you want from life or even a slice of the pie you have been desiring? I did not for a long time and guess what? I actually still manifested these things but would also self-sabotage and then end up having issues or losing them altogether. Finally, I figured out through other psychological work this was because I did not feel good enough or worthy of having what I wanted to begin with. Learn from my mistakes!

Notes – Thoughts – Ideas – Affirmations – Dreams

29 – Emotions Are The Key

"Emotions have immense power. This power can propel you towards your dreams and goals, or sabotage and ruin your life. Choose wisely how to use the power of your emotions." ~ Stan Jacobs, The Dusk & Dawn Master

GET EXCITED!

Your emotions are the fuel powering your thoughts being manifested into reality. This is key and a big part of doing this successfully. I can write on paper all day long that I now own my beautiful dream home in the perfect location for me, but if I do not feel a true desire and excitement behind that, it won't have enough gas to come to me very quickly or at all.

We all do not wake up each day excited. There are many stressors and items that are constantly tugging at us to put us in a less than desirable mood. You must take control of this. After all, this is your reality, so control it. Start by getting somewhere quiet, maybe with a cup of coffee, tea, or glass of water. Check in with yourself. How are you feeling as you awake? Acknowledge any feelings you have whether negative or positive. Take a yogi breath or two. Grumpy? Use sound to change that. You could walk outdoors where you hear nature sounds, put nature sounds on your mp3 player, or another musical choice that makes you feel happier or less stressed. Awhile later, pump up the beat with something more up tempo that makes you feel more energetic. Congratulations! You are being responsible. You are controlling the way you choose to

respond to your environment. This is major. Think of how many times you did not do this and your day just happened to you. Now, you are making the day happen. I am proud of you!

When you are working on visualizing your desires, emotions play an important part. You must write as if you own that car and feel the emotion you would feel putting the pedal to the metal.

Now, as a gift for holding your breath so many times, I am going to give you another trick.

Trick #2 – When you know it, you own it!

I recently spent some time helping my grandson with fractions. Some of the problems I gave him he said were "easy". Yes, well that is because you know this. You know how to do this. Another child or even adult may not know it and to them, it would seem hard." I told him I was going to help him discover some new things that right now seem hard, but it is only because he did not know them yet. "Once you know it, you own it and it is easy", I said. Thereon, we had a little saying: "When you know it, you own it". We would say this many times during the school work, laughing and smiling. This changed the emotional signature surrounding the task of fractions.

Perhaps you already know about conscious creation but have fallen away from doing it on purpose and with intention. If so, you know it and you can own it again. If this is your first experience with using your own mind and intent to consciously create your reality, it may seem difficult. I assure you it is easy and fun. You can do it. You are already doing it …. Just not with conscious intent most of the time.

Your feelings are the gasoline or fuel for your vibrational signature around your body/mind/spirit complex. The stronger an emotion is, the more validity it contains in your reality that is constantly being generated around you. It is

critical and wise to master this fact: the force, universe, God or whatever you want to call it — the manifestation machine does not differentiate between one end of the pole or another.

As I spoke of earlier with the law of attraction, one end of the pole can be hot and the other cool with warm in the middle. If your emotions run cold and that is the strongest feeling, your manifestations will tip toward that even if you actually desire the hot end of the stick. You have more emotion invested in the cold side and that is what will keep appearing for you. If your feelings are more intensely focused on what you do not want or what you fell you lack, more of that will show up. By having a strong "knowing" backed often only by faith in the unseen force, you will achieve the final outcome you desire — often better than what you originally envisioned.

It is important to fully know that our thoughts lead to our feelings. Thoughts we have generate emotions. This is why the more we can shut down our negative self-talk, the better. It is also why stating affirmations out loud with enthusiasm and high emotion helps erase at least ten negative thoughts. Mind exercises including guided visualization, positive daydreaming, meditation and hypnosis can assist us in reining in our negative thought patterns and changing them permanently.

To manifest really well, approach the situation with heightened emotions of excitement. Be diligent about the steps of minding your self talk, clearing negative patterns, forgiving yourself and others where needed, being grateful, and knowing you are worthy to have and ready to receive. It can seem like a lot of work, but with diligent practice, you will find it becomes more natural, running like a well oiled machine for you.

Have and cultivate faith. You will see things begin to manifest and synchronicities will begin to occur. This will deepen your faith in how reality creation works. Still, you may repeatedly have an overriding doubt such as does this really work? Keep going through all the steps with faith and high

emotion. These doubts will fade, especially as small and large things are manifested and you experience some beautiful synhronicities.

When we imagine something and fuel it with our intention and emotions, it becomes almost like a thought bubble above us. In fact, it is an invisible thought form we carry with us. The more we believe and affirm that our desire encapsulated in the thought bubble (or something better) will happen, the more strength it has to begin to bleed into visible reality. By creating our desires like this and allowing them to exist in a field around us, we can nurture them with an emotional expectancy that we know that or something greater will occur.

While we have been led to believe we are powerless or that fate owns our destiny … or that only God Source can create, this is untrue. My own experiments prove to myself this is not true. We have been given the ability to create and the gift of co-creating with this God Source and each other.

Threads and strands of thought are formed into an intelligent pattern of its own. We fuel and breathe life into it as we imagine it. As we further hold that thought and ride it like a horse onto its destination, it will come into this realm of existence. Resist the urge to put limitations of time or quantities on the desire. Instead, leave it open to those thoughts or something even better, knowing you have higher sources directing you toward your best good.

The energetic blueprint is built in the thought matrix. It has to be born — it has to come into its own fruition below. When your negative ego or another person or institution says it can't or won't happen, you have to basically think they are full of crap. You have to know and you can know. Once you have created and fueled this thought form, written it down as if it has already happened, lit the fire of desire, give gratitude to the universe for working with you to create it, it's yours. It is just

that simple and that is why this knowledge has remained secret or occult. To have everyone knowing or to teach them they are actually very powerful co-creators goes against the grain of ruling establishments who want to be able to exercise control over the people.

The positive ramifications here are enormous. We can learn by creating our own events and things to begin to master this creation process. We can begin to work in groups of two or more to hold and send out thoughts that impact in a positive way. Ultimately, we can join many others in person and through distance to achieve a loving harmonious state on our planet.

This is so achievable. You only have to be willing to begin. Like an infant who first must roll over, then sit up, crawl and walking within a year, you also can begin or resume this journey now and I would love for you to walk with me. Let's go together where the skies are blue, the earth is lush, there are no wars, and lies to the people no longer work. We are closer than you realize. In fact, it is only a few steps away.

The Steps

- Visualize - daydream with expanded emotion. Open up and allow the possibilities
- Open Your Eyes to everything around you - watch for clues, synchronicities. Be open to your desires happening. Watch for signs.
- Keep diet clean as possible. Limit heavy items such as meat, dairy. Utilize periods of cleansing toxins through fasting and other holistic modalities.
- Check your alignment or frequency often. Be in touch with your emotions and thoughts.

- Be or become the change you want. Become the person or energy who would attract your desires.
- Have patience. Events can happen fast or take some time as conditions line up to propel you toward your dreams and desires. Be mindful that all in nature runs in cycles.
- Meditate and clear your mind. Stay connected with God Source and listen

Practice being in the now and being mindful of your thoughts and feelings. Why is this useful as we hear it so often now? Staying present with what is right in front of you and not veering too far off into the future or past allows you to develop greater levels of concentration and focus. It also is a great way to take you away from a fear mode of thinking.

Often when we project into the future, it is out of worries, fear or anxiety. Some people can creatively visualize something wonderful far off in the future such as money — receiving large sums of cash. Then, they begin worrying about what to do with it, how to spend it, and who might try to take advantage of them if they have it. See what I am saying?

What if you creatively visualized you are sitting in your bedroom in the middle of all that cash? There you are, throwing it up in the air like confetti. Perhaps you see yourself sitting on the bed and counting the cash into neat piles. Perhaps, you see it as signing onto your bank account and you cannot believe how much money you have now in the bank. Anyway, you want to imagine it in the now is fine.

Another benefit of staying in the now is that you will take smaller steps on your manifesting journey, but each one will have more impact and leave a larger impact because it is extremely focused. As you hone in on your intentions for creating your destiny and keep your goals right in front of you, all will come to fruition much easier.

Build Your Future

We are constantly building our future from where our mind and actions are situated in the present. Periodically, examine these questions to constantly make sure what you are building is what you want.

- What are my thoughts radiating?
- What type of feelings fuel my thoughts?
- What do I find myself thinking of the most?
- Is there are dominating theme around my frequent thoughts?
- If I could name two things about what I believe strongly, what would it be?
- What do I feel like I need to believe in more deeply?
- What do I expect on a deep level to happen?
- What is easiest for me to imagine?
- Is there anything I wish I could visualize or imagine better or with more depth?
- Do I find myself fearful, worried or feeling doubtful at times? If so, over what?
- Which areas of my life am I the most positive about?
- Where do I expect good outcomes?

How much time per day or week am I spending?

A) meditating

B) visualizing - daydreaming

C) prayer

TOOLS

A vision board - poster board - collection of images on computer perhaps used as your wallpaper or screensaver - private board on Pinterest.

Box of Desires - Designate a special jar or box where you write down your desires on slips of paper and place them inside. Make sure you are writing the item or event as if it has already happened.

Book of Desires - Like the box method above, utilize a journal dedicated only to manifesting your desires. This is my favorite method that I have used successfully many times. Truly, things that seemed like they could not happen did occur just from writing it down as if it had already happened, reading it periodically with emotional feeling as if it had happened, and then later watching it unfold. Many times, my desire came into being at what almost seemed like the last opportunity for it to do so. Other times, it happened much swifter than I would imagine it could have. This is a powerful manifesting method when used correctly. There are no lengthy instructions. Simply identify what you truly want — write it down in the book as if it has already occurred; read it on some sort of regular basis with great enthusiasm. This is how it is done.

However, know that you should keep it general without too many specifics. In other words, I would not write down that "John has finally fallen in love with me and proposed marriage." You see, there may be a much better pairing for you than John — even though you cannot see that now. Instead, it would be wiser to write: "I now have a partner who loves me fully for who I am and we make our future together." This allows the Universe to serve you up something more delicious. It also keeps you from infringing upon the free will of John.

In this book, you have either gained knowledge or been reminded of principles you knew, but somehow were not using. Perhaps, you forgot some steps along the way. It is easy to

have that happen. I have created this end section that briefly summarizes, almost in a checklist fashion, so that when things seem to not be working out for you, you can return to this page and quickly examine the list. From that, you will hopefully be able to see which area(s) you still need to master.

Responsibility

Remember you are already creating your reality and manifesting people and situations around you. This is being done unknowingly, partial knowing yet haphazardly, or with full knowledge. Take responsibility and know that you need to begin focusing.

Reciprocity

Are you really prepared to have what you believe you want? Are you ready to receive? You have learned in this book about the reciprocity of giving and receiving and how you need to do both. Try to determine if you are more of a taker or a receiver. Once you have determined that, come up with ways to balance it out so both sides are more equal within yourself.

Desires Aligned With Body/Mind/Spirit

Birth your desires through the beautiful act of daydreaming. Just slip into that mind frame and determine what you truly desire in at least one area of your life. It may be something material such as a vehicle, vacation, new place to live. Perhaps you desire a romantic relationship and friendship with someone you can trust. You also want to be highly attracted to them and want lasting fulfillment. Whatever it is, daydream and ask that God Source help you make this happen. Holding desire in your mind and heart can be a very exhilarating experience. While daydreaming, conjure the

emotions you will feel when you have what you desire. Bring as much emotion and visual experience into the daydream as you can.

Timing

Many people give up because things do not happen or appear within a time frame they have predetermined. So often, if not every time, there is something else going on and it involves moving into a better desired creation than you originally intentioned. It is important to not worry about when things will occur. Instead, have an inner knowing that what you desire or something even better has already happened and soon you will see it revealed to you in this reality. It is that simple. Take that mind frame really to heart and believe it instead of torturing yourself about how it has not happened yet and probably will not.

Speaking of your heart, make a commitment of loyalty to yourself and your desires. As you step forward in heart-felt faith and stay loyal to your beliefs, this is at least fifty percent of the formula. It also requires you to stay open for the right conditions or opportunities and be a bit flexible with your original intention. Again, many times there is something better in store for you. Be tenacious, yet loose with how it all comes about for you.

Thoughts & Beliefs

Be very mindful of your thoughts and feelings regarding the subject matter of your desire. Work to actively remove any negative hindrances that linger there. Forgive yourself for these, stating "these are just old patterns that are worn out and ready to be replaced with my new emotions and thoughts." Work on that each day with affirmations.

Write down in your notebook or journal this desire as if it has already happened. Generate a thankful feeling inside and visualize yourself enjoying the situation.

Gratitude & Feelings

Once per day, generate a true feeling of gratitude for all the experiences you have now and the desire that is coming toward you. Write down one thing you are grateful for.

Believe when your feelings falter. Stop yourself and realize that all it takes is a little faith to move a mountain.

Reinforce it with visualizing or daydreaming about your desired outcome

When you get an intuitive feeling, follow it and if it leads to an opportunity, seize it and takc action.

Notes – Thoughts – Ideas – Affirmations – Dreams

30 – Till We Meet Again

"Happy trails to you, until we meet again. Some trails are happy ones, others are blue. It's the way you ride the trail that counts, here's a happy one for you." ~ Dale Evans

There is not a magic spell you can perform once, weekly, monthly or yearly to be the magical empath. You are the spell and all the information you have revisited again or gained over time demonstrates to you that living a magical life has some common components that must be adopted:

Good treatment of self

Regular devotion and practice

Balanced approach in daily living

Good treatment of others

Focus & Intention

Gratitude

Love and peace were words used as a mantra of the 1960's. Make love - not war was another frequent saying. Astrologically, we have now moved into a new era that affects the entire planet … the Age of Aquarius. With everything you have learned and are still learning, you have the ability to affect the peace, love and understanding in this world you live in.

Through meditation, visualization and wise choices and actions, you can save the world from a hateful, destructive demise.

Yet, know that you are immortal. Ends are always new beginnings. Ask God the Source of All to help make you a divine blessing to all whom you encounter on each realm where you exist — physical, mental and spiritual. Ask this daily and see how it transforms your world.

Yes, the entire world depends on you being responsible for your thoughts, feelings and actions. This extends to how you treat yourself and others. This is your hero or heroine journey and the fact that you sought this information you are absorbing and putting into practice confirms this. When you start treating yourself and truly seeing yourself as a powerful being cut from the cloth of God the Source, you will begin to transform your world into something more positive and full of life and love.

Staying focused is part of the challenge as you will have many distractions. Sometimes, our own ego initiates these events. Remember that all are made in the image of God The Source and all have a spark of divine within. Recognize and honor that. We are all included in the "All", yet not a single one of us is "the All".

If you build a house, the house is "The All." One nail that went into the house is part of it, but it is not the total house. Yet, each nail, beam and wall are integral parts of the house. Likewise, you are not God Source, but a part of it — an integral part helping to hold it all together and you have the opportunity to express this in a myriad of beneficial ways to improve the quality of The All.

Try to avoid being a rusty nail or a warped board. Stay strong and pass your strength to the entire house. Be grateful for things small and large. Let your strength be fueled by the wondrous power of gratitude which changes your physiology in an instant and ultimately will change your entire world.

With love, light and gratitude to you,

Lyra

Thank you for reading this second book in *The Magical Empath* series. I wish you continued success as you move magically along your path!

One of the best gifts you could give me is your written review of this work ☺

Visit
lyraadams.com and download unusual freebies

Notes – Thoughts – Ideas – Affirmations – Dreams

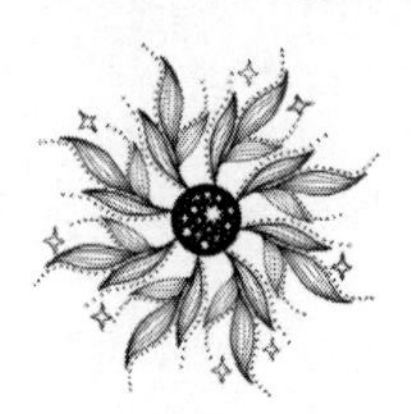

Bibliography

Emoto, Masaru. (2004). *Love Thyself: The Message From Water III.* Hay House Inc.

Etymonline. (2021). Retrieved from: https://www.etymonline.com/word/spell

Fluke. (2021). *What is Resistance?* Retrieved from: https://www.fluke.com/en-us/learn/blog/electrical/what-is-resistance

Iowa State University. N.D. *Physics of Nondestructive Evaluation – Electricity – Series Circuits*. Retrieved from: https://www.nde-ed.org/Physics/Electricity/index.xhtml

Merriam-Webster Dictionary. (2021). Retrieved from: https://www.merriam-webster.com/words-at-play/word-history-spell

Physics Stack Exchange. (2013). *Will current pass without any resistance?* Retrieved from: https://physics.stackexchange.com/questions/69919

Psychology Today. N.D. *Dark Triad.* Retrieved from: https://www.psychologytoday.com/us/basics/dark-triad

The Law of One (The Ra Material). (1982). Transcripts 88.13-16 and 93:16-17 retrieved from: https://www.lawofone.info. More resources also at https://www.llresearch.org

Made in United States
North Haven, CT
06 July 2023